You are about to start on an adventure which will reward you for the rest of your life . . .

If you find yourself in a situation where you seem to be going nowhere, feel inadequate and unable to face life with enthusiasm and confidence, *this book is for you*. If you are disgusted with mediocrity and not content to just drift through life, these pages offer you an alternative. If you can make yourself open and receptive to new concepts, values and beliefs, you will discover how you can systematically reorganize your thought processes to awaken THE NEW YOU.

It makes no difference who you are, what you do or what your life situation is, YOU can achieve total self-confidence!

Y0-CAV-232

THE ULTIMATE SECRETS OF
TOTAL SELF-CONFIDENCE

DR. ROBERT ANTHONY

BERKLEY BOOKS, NEW YORK

This Berkley book contains the complete
text of the original edition.
It has been completely reset in a typeface
designed for easy reading, and was printed
from new film.

THE ULTIMATE SECRETS OF TOTAL SELF-CONFIDENCE

A Berkley Book / published by arrangement with
New Thought Publications

PRINTING HISTORY
New Thought edition published 1979
Berkley edition / September 1984
Second printing / January 1985
Third printing / May 1985
Fourth printing / November 1985

ISBN: 0-425-09143-0

A BERKLEY BOOK ® TM 757,375
Berkley Books are published by The Berkley Publishing Group,
200 Madison Avenue, New York, New York 10016.
The name "BERKLEY" and the stylized "B" with design
are trademarks belonging to Berkley Publishing Corporation.

PRINTED IN THE UNITED STATES OF AMERICA

Acknowledgements

No author ever writes a book alone. I have drawn the ideas from many sources including, of course, my own experiences in lecture work and private practice. People in the field of psychology, religion and metaphysics have assisted me. Many prefer to remain anonymous, content with the fact that their knowledge and experience may help someone gain spiritual and psychological freedom.

It would be difficult to acknowledge everyone from whom I have borrowed ideas but I insist on thanking a few by name. I have been profoundly influenced by Anthony Norvell, my personal teacher and counselor; Marguerite & Willard Beecher for their excellent work in helping others to develop self-reliance; Lilburn Barksdale for his outstanding program and booklets on self-esteem; and the writings of Maxwell Maltz, Joseph Murphy, Emmet Fox, Abraham Maslow, Ralph Waldo Emerson, Napolean Hill, and Ernest Holmes.

Robert Anthony

Dedication

To every person who wishes to improve the quality of his or her life, I acknowledge you for taking the time to buy and read this book. The time and effort sets you apart from the majority. As you become aware of your unlimited possibilities for creation you will not only prosper and develop yourself but you will gain a great wealth of information that will allow you to help others who can follow your example.

Table of Contents

Introduction

THE UNHAPPY MAJORITY

As you look around at your fellow human beings, you will find it hard to ignore the fact that very few people are happy, fulfilled and leading purposeful lives. Most of them seem unable to cope with their problems and the circumstances of daily living. The majority, settling for the average, have resigned themselves to "just getting by." Resignation to mediocrity has become a way of life. As a result, feelings of inadequacy cause them, quite humanly, to blame society, people, circumstances, and surrounding conditions for their failures and disappointments. The idea that people and things control their lives is so thoroughly ingrained in their thinking that they normally will not respond to logical arguments which prove otherwise.

William James, the eminent philosopher and psychologist, once observed that the greatest discovery of our age has been that we, by changing the inner aspects of our thinking, can change the outer aspects of our lives. Wrapped up in this brief statement is the dynamic truth that we are *not victims but co-creators* in the building of our lives and the world around us. Or, as another sage puts it, we aren't what we think we are, but what *we think,* we are!

THE SHEEP STATE OF MIND

A lesson which has taken us far too long to learn is that the opposite of bravery is not cowardliness but conformity. You may have spent valuable, irreplaceable years trying to fit into the parade only to learn, too late, that the people you have been following have been following you! This is particularly evident in the timing of our lives' major events.

What makes us follow each other like sheep? Why should one marry, for instance, or graduate, or settle down, or do anything else when one's friends do? Perhaps these events don't belong in our lives until much later. Perhaps they even belonged earlier. Perhaps they don't belong at all.

Let's get out of this sheep state of mind and refuse to punish ourselves because we are different from our neighbor or associates. Much suffering would be eliminated if we could assert our Divine right as individuals and refuse to let the sacredness and beauty of life be marred by conformity or standardization.

THE EMPHASIS IS ON THE INDIVIDUAL

To *think* that your life is controlled *in any way* by another individual, group, or society imposes a condition of mental slavery which makes you a prisoner by your own decree. Your thoughts become the blueprints which attract from your subconscious mind all the elements that go into fulfilling your concepts, whether they be positive or negative. What you have in your life right now is the outward manifestation of what has been going on in your mind. You have literally *attracted* everything that has come into your life, good or bad, happy or sad, success or failure. And this includes all facets of experience be it business, marriage, health or personal affairs.

Think of it! Your surroundings, your environment, your world all outwardly picture what you think about inwardly. By discovering why you are the way you are, you also find the key to be what you want to be.

YOU HAVE THE POWER TO CHANGE

Shakespeare said, "We know what we are, but not what we may be."

Does this describe you? Do you concentrate on your limitations, your failures, your blundering way of doing things, seldom stopping to think of what you might be? The problem is that you have been conditioned since childhood by false concepts, values and beliefs which have prevented you from realizing how truly capable and unique you are.

By virtue of your role as co-creator of your life, you have the power to change any of its aspects. Every great teacher has come to the same conclusion: you cannot look to someone outside yourself to solve your problems. As the Master Teacher reminded us so often, "The Kingdom of Heaven is within you." It's not in some distant land, and it's not up in the sky. Buddha came to the same realization when he said, "Be a lamp unto your own feet and do not seek outside yourself." Self-healing powers are within. Health, happiness, abundance and peace of mind are *natural* states of being once you break the bonds of negative thinking.

Unless you perceive your own true worth as a person, you cannot come close to achieving total self-confidence. Only to the degree that you can truly acknowledge your own unique importance will you be able to free yourself from self-imposed limitations. Yes, I said *self-imposed!* Your parents, your family, your boss or society didn't do it to you. You did it to yourself by *allowing* others to control your life.

If you can't get rid of your guilt feelings and cease belittling yourself for your imagined inadequacies, you will be one of those who continue the fruitless struggle to attain total self-confidence and personal freedom. In order to be truly free, compassionate, warm and loving, you must first start by understanding and loving yourself. To follow Luke's admonition, "To love thy neighbor as thyself," without beginning with a full appreciation of who and what *you* are, defrauds both you and your neighbor!

FULFILLING YOUR NEEDS FIRST

One of the principal requisites for change, and a self-confident personality is that you must satisfy your own needs first. It is not your job to please others first no matter who may have told you that. On the surface this may appear selfish, but let's remind ourselves of St. Luke's comment that only when we have done our best to make the most of ourselves can we be of greatest service to our families, friends, churches, communities, etc.

Many people use the philosophy of service to others first as an escape from taking responsibility for changing their lives. They say that their husbands or wives must come first; their boyfriends or girlfriends; their churches or families or the world must come first. This is nothing but self-deception. An example of this kind of behavior is the person who buries himself sacrificially in a commendable project with missionary zeal when, in truth, he can't face and eliminate his own problems.

Dr. Seabury in his *Art of Selfishness* says, "Don't worry about the whole world: if you do, it will overwhelm you. Worry about one wave at a time. Please yourself. Do something for you, and the rest will fall into line."

You can't change the world, but you *can* change *yourself*. The only way the human situation will improve is for each individual to take charge of his or her own life in a positive, constructive manner. The time has come for you to stop everything else and give total priority to your needs first. This is the only way you'll ever be free. Physical slavery is a punishable crime but, far worse, is mental slavery for the punishment is, as Descartes put it so well, "A life of quiet desperation."

COME ABOARD! IT'S TAKE-OFF TIME!

You are about to start on an adventure which will reward you for the rest of your life. You are going to learn new ways to break the bonds of limitation that have been holding you back.

If you find yourself in a situation where you seem to be going nowhere, feel inadequate and unable to face life with enthusiasm and confidence, this book is for you. If you are disgusted with mediocrity, disappointed by past results and not content to just drift through life, these pages offer you an alternative. If you can make yourself open and receptive to new concepts, values and beliefs, you will discover why you should and how you can systematically reorganize your thought processes to awaken *THE NEW YOU*. Once you master these principles, you will have more happiness, more love, more freedom, more money and more self-confidence than you ever thought possible. Nothing is more rewarding in life than releasing your unlimited potential and leading a creative, purposeful life. It makes no difference who you are, what you do or what your life situation is, *YOU* can achieve total self-confidence. And the approach is not nearly as complicated as you might think!

GET THE 21 DAY HABIT

Let's slip backstage for a moment and steal a glimpse at a simple but very effective learning technique. It is called THE 21 DAY HABIT.

It has been determined that it takes approximately twenty-one days to break an old, destructive habit or form a new, positive habit. It will take you at least that long to fully absorb the material in this book. Make no mistake. You will *understand* it immediately, but intellectual understanding alone will get you nowhere, and will not change your behavior. The real thrill comes when, at last, you learn to follow your "knows."

Following your "knows" means that you must go from initial understanding to *knowing*. In order to *know* something, it must become part of your thinking, feeling, actions and reactions. And this takes time. So don't make the mistake of just reading the book once and saying, "I know it!" You won't "know it" until it has been absorbed into your consciousness and becomes a new habit pattern.

Put everything aside for a while and apply your full concentration to what you read. The hours spent in changing your negative, self-defeating habit patterns to positive, constructive ones will be a small investment compared to the rewarding return of a lifetime of accomplishment and freedom.

To obtain the best results, read the book through once and familiarize yourself with the entire scope of the material. Then return to the specific chapters which will help in solving your immediate problems. Let the principles sink deeply into your consciousness and, most importantly, ACT upon them without delay.

Now, if you are ready, let's get going!

THE
ULTIMATE
SECRETS OF

TOTAL SELF-CONFIDENCE

Secret #1
DEHYPNOTIZING YOURSELF

Every person has been hypnotized to some degree either by ideas he has accepted from others or ideas he has convinced himself are true. These ideas have exactly the same effect upon his behavior as those implanted into the mind of a hypnotic subject by a professional hypnotist. In my lecture work, I have hypnotized hundreds of people to demonstrate the power of suggestion and imagination. To best illustrate my point, let me explain what happens when a person is hypnotized.

Under hypnosis, I tell a normal, healthy woman who weighs 120 pounds that she cannot lift a pencil which is placed on a table. And, surprisingly, she finds herself unable to perform this simple act. It is not a question of her not *trying* to lift the pencil. She'll struggle and strain, much to the audience's amusement, but she simply *cannot* lift the pencil. On the one hand, she is trying to perform the action through voluntary effort and the use of her body muscles but, on the other, the suggestion that "you cannot lift the pencil" causes her *mind to believe* that it is *impossible*. Here we find a physical force being neutralized by a mental force. It is a case of will power versus imagination. When this happens, *imagination always wins out*.

Many people think they can change their lives through sheer will power. This is not true. Negative ideas in the imagination cause such persons to defeat themselves. Regardless of how hard they try, it's no use. They have accepted a false belief as if it were fact. All their ability, good intentions, effort and will power are of no avail against the powerful false belief they have accepted as truth.

In the same manner, I quickly prove that there is no limit to what a person can or cannot do when he or she is hypnotized because the power of imagination is limitless. To observers, I appear to have magical power to make her able and willing to do things she could not or would not ordinarily do. The truth is, of course, that the power is inherent in the subject. Without realizing it, my subject hypnotized herself into believing that she could or could not do these things. *No one can be involuntarily hypnotized as each person collaborates in the hypnotizing process.* The professional hypnotist is only a guide who helps the subject accelerate the phenomenon.

I have introduced this simple demonstration of hypnosis to illustrate a psychological principle which can be of great value to you. This same principle is becoming increasingly evident in the modern educational process where the student, in effect, actually educates himself with the skilled assistance of the teacher. And, even more dramatically, in the healing arts where the patient heals his own body under the professional guidance of a qualified physician or practitioner.

Once a person *believes* that something is true, whether or not it is, he then *acts* as if it were. He will instinctively seek to collect facts to support the belief no matter how false it may be. No one will be able to convince him otherwise unless, through personal experience or study, he is ready to change. Hence, it is easy to see that, if one accepts something which is not true, *all subsequent actions and reactions will be based upon a false belief.*

This is not a new idea. Since the beginning of time, both men and women have been in a kind of hypnotic sleep of which they were unaware but which has been recognized by great teachers and thinkers throughout the centuries. These people have perceived that humankind limits itself though its "mistaken certainties" and have sought to awaken us to our potential for greatness which goes far beyond anything we can possibly imagine.

It is, therefore, of utmost importance that *you not assume you are awake to the truth about yourself.* Said another way, you must not assume that what you now hold as truth is, in fact, really the Truth. Instead, you must proceed with the idea that you are presently hypnotized by false beliefs, concepts and values that are keeping you from being totally self-confident. It may be astutely observed at this point that you and I are primarily the result of what we have been told and taught; what we have been sold and bought.

The average person never comes near reaching his unlimited potential because he is living under the false assumption that he already *knows* the truth. He believes what his parents have told him, what his teachers have taught him, what he has read, and what his religion preaches WITHOUT ACTUALLY PROVING ANYTHING FOR HIMSELF. Millions upon millions of people have blindly followed the rhetoric of so-called "knowledgeable people" without making sure that the principles these "experts" expound stand up to the realities of life. They further limit themselves by holding onto these concepts, values and beliefs even after they have actually evolved beyond them. Fortunately, something or someone has triggered *your* interest in higher horizons which includes the discovery and development of a totally self-confident personality.

Your first job is to *awaken* from the hypnotic condition that is presently keeping you from being the person you want to be. Read the following statement and MARK IT WELL:

The degree to which you awaken will be in direct proportion to the amount of truth you can accept about yourself.

Now read it again! This is the key which determines how much you will be able to change your life. In the words of the Master Teacher, "Know the Truth and the Truth shall set you free."

Many of the concepts presented in this book will be in direct opposition to what you now hold as the Truth. Some may even seem "way out" or illogical. These will so challenge your viewpoints that you will either read them and say, "This is worth experimenting with," or you will flatly refuse to accept them. This brings us back to what we said earlier: *your life will be transformed in direct relation to the amount of truth you can accept about yourself.* No better advice was ever given us than, "With all thy getting, get understanding."

If you are sincere about changing your life for the better, you must have an open mind. You must learn to understand what is being said without the necessity of believing it. I neither want nor expect you to accept as true anything you read in this book, just because I say it's true. If you do, you will gain little from the material. You must try out the principles for yourself. The inner conviction and security, which comes from having proved *to your own satisfaction* that what is presented as the Truth is indeed really the Truth, is the foundation upon which to begin building a dynamic self-confident personality.

In order to construct a new 'functional' building on a site where one that is "inefficient" exists, you first have to raze the old structure. This must be done by shattering those "mistaken certainties" which have held you back from expressing the unlimited, abundant, wholesome life you desire. This is primarily what this book is about.

HOW YOUR BELIEFS
IMPRISON YOU

Just what are beliefs? They are the conscious and unconscious information that we have accepted as true which fill our structure and form the basis for our behavior patterns and ethics. Our beliefs imprison us and deny us access to what is *real*. A filter of misconceptions prohibits truth's passage and we see *only what we want*, and reject everything else.

Truth can never be revealed to the so-called "firm believer." You know the type: always quoting "facts." He does not want to recognize anything outside of his beliefs and sees everything with which he disagrees as a threat. He goes through life labeling all that is new, different and enlightening as "evil" or, at least "unacceptable," and all that is old, traditional and suppressing as "good." He cannot understand that Truth—no matter how painful—is always, by its very nature, "good," and that a lie—regardless of how much we are in love with it—is always, by its very nature, "bad."

To protect his beliefs, he builds a wall around his world. Some "firm believers" have a big wall and some a small one but, regardless of the size of the structure, it can only serve to shut out more of the Truth than it can hold.

The person who is a "firm believer" has no option to change his mind. This makes him ignorant. He can only recognize what lies *within* the walls he has built around himself and is prevented from exploring the limitless Truth which lies outside the wall. What he fails to realize is that Truth is always greater than any structure built to contain it.

Belief and faith are not the same thing and should not be confused. Unlike belief, faith is not totally limiting. It recognizes there is much to discover and know, and that one must always seek to unfold more and more of the Truth. With faith, *all things are possible*. The "firm believer" always thinks he knows the answer. The person with faith, aware that he knows very little, constantly seeks enlightenment.

YOU ARE LIMITED BY YOUR "MISTAKEN CERTAINTIES"

If you wish to make a fundamental change in your life, you must first understand the root of your problems. This invariably lies in your "mistaken certainties."

Mistaken certainties are things you are sure are true but which, in fact, are not. They are generally based on *wishful thinking* which distorts reality and leads to self-deception. We want things to be as we would *like* them to be rather than as they are. We look at the world through rose-colored glasses which permit our wish for the ideal to blind us to what is *real*.

You can only change the world to the extent that you can change *yourself*. And you can only change yourself to the degree that you become aware of your mistaken certainties. Most of your troubles arise from expectations which have not become realities. And most of your disappointments from your mistaken ideal of what you think you *"should,"* or *"ought"* to *do*, or *be*, according to your present level of awareness. This is known as *resisting reality*.

Emerson said, "We are what we think about all day long." Everything that is happening to you right now in your mental, physical, emotional and spiritual world is the result of what is going on in your mind. To put it more exactly:

You accept, relate or reject EVERYTHING in your mental and physical environment on the basis of your PRESENT level of AWARENESS.

Your present level of awareness is determined by your education, environment, family life, childhood experiences, successes, failures and religious beliefs.

You will discover that many of the things you thought were true are the things that, in reality, are *not true*. These will include the beliefs which make up the solid foundation of what you *assumed* was reality. As you progress, you will discover that everything you were accepting, relating or rejecting was done on the basis of a level of awareness *which may have been faulty or distorted*.

NO ONE LIKES TO CHANGE THEIR PRESENT LEVEL OF AWARENESS

Let's face it! We all find it difficult to change our present levels of awareness because—

1. What we are picturing and imagining in our minds is based on what we now believe is the Truth, regardless of how faulty or distorted it may be. Our minds control our actions and reactions.
2. It is easier to give excuses or, as we prefer to call them, 'logical reasons' why it isn't necessary or even possible to change.
3. We seek only those experiences which support our present scale of values and avoid, resist or, if necessary, forcibly reject those which are inconsistent with our existing beliefs.

4. We have built and programmed into our subconscious minds and central nervous systems the wrong responses to life situations and we respond the way we have been programmed. In other words, we respond to the way we have been conditioned to FEEL and ACT. The "system" is one of our *own creations* and only we can change its basic patterns.

Intellectually, we may agree that we should change but we almost always feel that our situation is different from everyone else's. We avoid, resist and, if necessary, forcibly reject any idea which threatens our beliefs. Take, for example, the alcoholic. From his viewpoint of life it seems rational to continue drinking. The drug user, the compulsive gambler and the compulsive eater all feel the same way about their respective "addictions." They rationalize their actions based on *their present level of awareness*, however faulty it may be.

The major stumbling block to changing our faulty awareness is that we do not want to recognize and accept *reality*, or *what is*, because our "mistaken certainties" have distorted our perception. This is why it is important, from time to time, to challenge our beliefs to see if we are operating from the wrong viewpoint. This is one lesson we can take from the Good Book which repeatedly challenges us to, "Prove me now herewith!"

The beliefs of a person who has a normal, wholesome personality undergo a constant process of reorganization, but the neurotic personality clings to his beliefs, false and distorted though they may be. Usually the only way the neurotic will change is when a major crisis forces him to alter his old self-defeating habit patterns.

If your mind has been programmed or conditioned to believe false and distorted concepts and values, you will develop a lifestyle to justify them. You will assume that something is reality even though it is false. Then, *seeking to prove you are right*, you will collect and make the facts fit. You become like a dog chasing its tail. One false belief leads to another until you can no longer function rationally. Here is what Prescott Lecky, one of the great pioneers of self-image psychology, has to say about this.

> *Neurotic behavior is a reflection of the fact that the individual strives to maintain the nuclear composition acquired in childhood and in early life, behaving in accordance with immature attitudes and resisting conflicting new experiences which would tend to force personality reorganization. Although normal people undergo a constant process of nuclear reorganization with enrichment of experiences, the neurotic personality clings to unhealthy and unrealistic organizations of ideas which may require external intervention to affect needed reorganization.*

YOUR NUMBER ONE PRIORITY

Your number one priority in life is your own well-being and *the expansion of your awareness*. By expanding your awareness, you will remove the "mistaken certainties" which have been keeping you from being the self-confident person you would like to be. You do this by:

1. Ceasing to automatically and arbitrarily defend your personal viewpoints of "right" and "wrong." Defending them makes you unteachable and blocks the reception of new ideas. You must learn to screen the entries but still keep the door ajar.
2. Reassessing your concepts, values, beliefs, ideals, assumptions, defenses, aggressions, goals, hopes and compulsions.
3. Reorganizing and understanding your real *needs* and *motivations*.
4. Learning to trust your intuition.
5. Observing your mistakes and trying to correct them; being aware that herein lie some of the most valuable lessons you'll ever learn.
6. Loving yourself and others.
7. Learning to listen without prejudging and automatically thinking, "This is good;" "that is bad." Training yourself to listen to WHAT is being said without the necessity of believing it.
8. Noticing what you are defending most of the time.
9. Realizing that your new awareness will provide you with the means and motivation to change for the better.

Begin to ask yourself, "Is my belief *rational*?" "Could I be mistaken?" If another person held that belief, you would be able to be very objective. You would, no doubt, present a convincing case why it was wrong. View your own beliefs in this manner. Question EVERYTHING and draw your own conclusions based on available evidence.

There is a positive answer only when the individual is willing to fulfill the demands of rigorous self-ex-

*amination and self-knowledge. If he follows through
his intention, he will not only discover some important
truth about himself, but will have gained a psychological advantage. He will set his hand, as it were,
to a declaration of his own human dignity and taken
the first step towards the foundation of his consciousness.*

—Carl Jung

WHY YOU CAN CHANGE

The startling point of all change is when we change the
DOMINANT BELIEFS which have been limiting our
awareness. It is possible to do this because *we make our
own world*.

Change is affected through our subconscious mind and
imagination. As Professor James pointed out, it begins with
changing *the inner aspects of our thinking*. We know, from
experience, that an outward change will come *after* we
change from *within*. By changing our DOMINANT
THOUGHTS OR BELIEFS, we change our awareness and,
hence, our reactions to people, circumstances and conditions.

In the familiar story of *Alice Through The Looking Glass*,
Alice had a problem. Before she could understand her new
world, she had to accept *new truths* about old, familiar
things. She had to make adjustments to her new world. If
you remember the story, she met some playing cards. She
observed that the playing cards had two sides. If she wanted

to really know the whole person, she had to see both sides of the cards. In other words, she had to get the TOTAL PICTURE. This is the way it must be with your life.

Before you can change your life to a more positive experience, you have to get the TOTAL PICTURE of yourself. You have to see yourself as others see you and your present world as it really IS, not as you wish it were. Then you are ready to start building that bridge between where you are now and where you'd like to be, and from what you are now to what you'd like to become.

> *The first reason for man's inner slavery is his ignorance, and above all, his ignorance of himself. Without self-knowledge, without understanding the workings and function of his machine, man cannot be free, he cannot govern himself, he will always remain a slave, the plaything of forces acting upon him. This is why in all ancient teachings the first demand at the beginning of the way to liberation was to "Know Thyself."*
>
> —*Gurdjieff*

Up to now, your greatest problem has been ignorance of yourself: both who you are and who you were meant to be. The wrong self-image has kept you from releasing your unlimited potential. You are like a bird in a cage which has no idea of how much vast space exists outside. Your 'mistaken certainties' have prevented you from realizing how truly worthy, capable and unique you are.

Secret #2
BONDAGE OR LIBERTY?

A self-confident personality is not possible until you have built a solid foundation of self-reliance. Many people think that a person who is self-reliant must be aloof, disinterested or unfriendly towards others. This is a totally false conception. By not being dependent, the self-reliant person can relate to others with compassion and empathy while, at the same time, retaining self-confidence and poise. Able to stand on his own two feet, he does not feel the need to manipulate others.

The main deterrent to self-reliance is the mistaken certainty that others are smarter, wiser or more intelligent than we are. And, so, we look to them for our happiness and welfare. The person who is dependent in this sense must always reach out to something external. He wants people, circumstances, conditions or God to do for him what he should be doing for himself. This causes him to depend, manipulate, conform, compare and compete.

In this chapter, we shall learn how these destructive habits act as deterrents to building a self-confident personality and how its release *demands* that you become *totally* self-reliant. But, first, a word about self-reliance.

SELF-RELIANCE

Self-reliance is not only the belief that you can handle things and become successful, it is something more than that. It is having the courage to listen to inner promptings for a hint of the kind of success you *should* want. It means taking your cue from what you are—not listening to something outside yourself—to get an idea of what you should become. When we learn to read the "signs" correctly and follow the kind of life that the urgings of our talents and temperaments tell us to pursue, we are happy and successful. We are ourselves and we are strong.

RECOGNIZING AND BREAKING THE DEPENDENCY HABIT

Dependency is slavery by mutual agreement. It is degrading for both the person who is dependent and the person who is being depended upon. Both parties are equally lacking in self-reliance for such a relationship flourishes on mutual exploitation.

The most unfortunate aspect of dependency is that when you think you are dependent on another individual—you are! You have neglected to develop the necessary self-reliance to meet and solve your own problems.

A sure sign of dependency is when you habitually *look up* to others as superior. The moment you begin to compare yourself with *anyone* you are subjecting yourself to psychological slavery.

The habit of leaning and depending is so ingrained in certain individuals that they abdicate all personal authority in favor of another person, philosophy or religion. They feel that they will be secure if they can find someone or some organization which is stronger and more knowledgeable than they and to whom or which they may cling with blind devotion. They allow this person, group or religion to be responsible for their happiness. And, of course, this includes the luxury of having someone or something to blame whenever failure occurs.

The leaning, dependent individual is at the mercy of those around him. Believing others smarter than himself, he is always looking for someone to lean on when a new problem confronts him. Subordinate to those upon whom he depends, their advice becomes a *command* which he feels compelled to follow. And where, as is frequently the case, there are several "advisors," he is in a constant state of exhaustion as he tries to decide whose advice to follow.

Advice is everywhere. Most of it is free and not worth the price. You usually have a dozen or more unpaid advisors who are more than happy to give you their opinion. But since others are generally engrossed in their own problems and do not know what you really "should," "ought" or "must" do, you invariably get the wrong advice. Indeed, accepting advice from someone who is not qualified to dispense it is like going to a plumber to get your teeth fixed. Most people can't solve their own problems so how can they advise you to do what they haven't been able to accomplish themselves?

Overcoming dependency isn't easy. We have been conditioned since childhood to look to others for our welfare, guidance and wisdom. But while dependency plays a role in our upbringing and education, it was never intended to obliterate individual identity. Each one of us is born with the innate ability to resolve whatever difficulties we face.

Read this and mark it well. NO ONE CAN EVER LET YOU DOWN IF YOU HAVEN'T BEEN LEANING ON THEM. No one can hurt your feelings, make you unhappy, lonely, angry or disappointed if you are not dependent on them for your welfare, inspiration, love or motivation.

The person who is self-reliant does not need to find a master to lean on. He is able to meet life's challenges with confidence and power by looking at each situation in the light of *reality*. He sees things as they *are*, not as he would like them to be and refuses to let his life be dominated by the habit of wishful thinking.

Once you have developed self-reliance, you do not have to procrastinate, escape or evade what is facing you because you have the confidence to meet each life situation with self-assurance and poise. You are free from worry because you know that you are in full control. You are not separated from your source of Power. You do not need repeated doses of inspiration and stimulation from others to do what you have to when motivation comes from within. You go through life with the realization that the internal Power is greater than any problem which faces you.

OVERCOMING THE NEED TO MANIPULATE

As a child, you neither knew nor cared about what was going on in the world around you. Your only concern was your own welfare. Helplessness made you dependent on what others would give and do for you. Your greatest happiness was being fed, held and fondled; your main concern was to get as much attention as possible.

You quickly discovered that, if you started to cry, you could summon an adult to take care of your needs. Even if you just got bored, you could start crying and someone would usually appear to comfort you. Smiling, too, worked exceptionally well. So you soon learned to smile when you were picked up and cry when you were put down.

This simple exercise in manipulation set the pace for the rest of your life. Your entire childhood was spent developing skills that would make a good impression on others and influence them to pay attention to you. Thus it was that, even at this early point in your life, you were programming yourself to depend on other people's approval and feel rejected when they disapproved. As a child, behavior like this was excusable but, as an adult, it's degrading. If you are still trying to manipulate others *to do that which you are sufficiently capable of doing yourself*, you cannot consider yourself emotionally mature.

A growing habit in our culture is to do more and more for children and expect less and less. Parents guilty of this are unwittingly cheating their offspring by allowing them to be dependent for things they should be doing for themselves. By spending their first eighteen years leaning and depending, children are cast in the role of prisoners with good behavior privileges. It is interesting to note that this is a human phenomenon. Shortly after birth, all other species of animal push their young out into the world where they soon learn independence.

The greatest gift any parent can give their children is to help them to become self-confident by making them self-reliant. Children should be given as much responsibility as they can handle at any age level. Only through independence will they learn the joy and privilege and human dignity of standing on their own two feet!

It is a basic responsibility of parents to assist children in making a smooth transition from dependency to self-reliance. In the transitional process, children should be allowed to make mistakes. Over-protection is wrong. If they are going to fall, let them. They will benefit from the experience. Spilling a glass of water shouldn't be a major catastrophe. If it is, small wonder that, in later life, when they must do something on their own, they say, "I can't do it!"

Unless they are sure of the outcome, they refuse to attempt anything because over-protective parents have always cushioned the way.

Every time you do something that someone is sufficiently capable of doing for themselves, you are literally stealing from that person. The more you care for someone, the more alert you must be to see that you are not depriving them of the opportunity to *think* and *do* for themselves, whatever the physical or emotional consequences. This is true not only in parent-child relationships but in marriage, family and all interpersonal relationships as well. We cannot live other people's lives or bear their burdens, no matter how much we love them.

The umbilical cord should be cut when children reach their early teens. They should be required to find *their own living quarters* no later than the age of eighteen or upon completing high school. Many parents will rebel against this idea with what, to them, seem to be logical reasons. But the fact still remains that nothing builds more self-reliance in a young adult than having to live alone. Without attempting to infer then this is the only reason, almost without exception the people who have achieved outstanding success in all fields of endeavor, including business, government, arts and sciences, are people who either were separated from their parents through hardship or decided to emancipate themselves in their young adult years.

We hear such excuses as, "We want to help them through school." "It will help them financially to live at home." "It's just until they get going." "They can't possibly afford their own place *and* go to school," etc. etc. The other side of the coin says, "I want control over my children's lives."

Parents who accept and cultivate this attitude only delay

and make more difficult the ultimate day of decision when their children must face the adult world on their own. Through the mistaken use of parental love, they have encouraged their offspring to continue to lean, depend and expect to receive help and support from others as if they were still small children.

Now, let's get our perspective here. We are not saying that you should not help or give to your child, husband or family. What we are saying is that you must allow them the individual freedom *to do what they feel they must* in order to grow and develop. Assisting them is where the giving comes in. Give them love, encouragement and recognition for their accomplishments. These are the vital elements of growth which they cannot supply for *themselves*. Financial assistance should only be offered if provision is made for its ultimate repayment.

Individuals who have not developed self-reliance have no alternative but to use manipulation to get what they want. If you are not self-reliant, you have to depend on your skill at influencing people to serve you and fulfill your needs. If you do use others as a vehicle to get through life, you cannot possibly go faster or further than you can convince them to take you. And, remember, if you are a parent, always be aware of any actions that will cause your child to remain in bondage because he or she will pay dearly for this type of behavior.

THE FATAL DECISION OF CONFORMITY

Most of us grew up never having to make any major decisions. Adults frequently deprived us of this responsibility and made them for us. If we tried to make a decision or state an opinion, it was never given any importance. Our parents were the final authority. We either agreed to their demands or else tried to talk our way out of what they wanted us to do.

As we entered adolescence, it became apparent that we would soon have to decide what was best for us. This can be a frightening experience as the average teenager goes forth into the adult world with very little preparation for what lies ahead. Our home training and system of education have largely ignored this vital and necessary part of our growth.

It is at this stage of our lives that we make the fatal decision to conform. As children, we were trained to obey or suffer the consequences so it is little wonder that, as we enter adulthood, most of us choose to perpetuate conformity as the easiest and most expedient approach to life. We prefer not to rock the boat because our need for approval is usually far stronger than our desire to do what we really want.

Conformity is one of the greatest psychological evils of humankind. The person caught in this destructive habit never does anything worthwhile with his life. He wants to be a great person, independent and do important things. But he can't. His motivation to always be approved of prevents him.

The conformist is filled with the need for approval. He can never get *enough*. He runs from one person to another seeking compliments and endorsements for his behavior and actions. As a child, he turned to parents and teachers; when he started to work, to his boss and fellow workers; in marriage, he turned to his mate. He must always have someone around to pat him on the head and tell him he is doing a good job. This bolsters up his poor self-esteem. By constantly seeking approval, he escapes from the responsibility of creating his own success and happiness and becomes totally dependent on others for his well-being. Indeed, he is their psychological slave; a person who can no longer imagine what life would be like if he approached it in a self-reliant manner.

Remember what we said earlier? The opposite of bravery is not cowardice but conformity. We should never invest another human being with the power to either build or wreck our lives, or dominate our initiative.

HOW COMPARISON BREEDS FEAR

Comparison is a sign of poor self-esteem. The person who compares himself to others lives in a state of fear. He fears those he imagines are above him. Believing them to be smarter, he feels unable to stand his ground. He fears those he imagines are below him because they seem to be catching up. If he works in a large company, he is always looking around him to see who is looming as a threat. The greater the height to which he rises, the greater his fear of falling.

The only way to get through life, he concludes, is to beat people at their own game. But, as his primary concern becomes being "one up" on the next person on his imaginary ladder, life loses its enjoyment.

COMPETITION—KILLER OF CREATIVITY

All forms of competition are hostile. They may seem friendly on the surface but the prime motivation is to be or do *"better than"* the next person. You were placed on this earth to *create*, not to compete, so if competition is used as your basic motivation to do anything, it will literally conspire against you and defeat you every time. What we're saying is that the purpose of life is to BE, not to compete. As one teacher puts it, "I'm *for* me, not *against* anyone!"

Although it may appear that the world is a competitive place, it is only competitive to those who feel the need to compete. Most people will reject this idea because of their childhood training where competition was rated right up there with apple pie and the American flag. If you ask them if they think competition is healthy, they will reply, with great enthusiasm, that it is not only healthy but necessary! They feel that it gives life meaning, purpose and direction; that a person needs a reward for doing a "good job." *It never occurs to them that the reward is in the doing and not in the end result.*

We compete with others only when we are unsure of ourselves and our abilities. *Competition is merely imitation.* It originates in early childhood from our need to copy others. The competitive person feels that others are better than he and sets out to prove otherwise. He struggles to surpass those he feels are superior. In effect, he is always comparing himself to people around him. The competitive person always needs someone else to validate how well he is doing.

The self-reliant individual, on the other hand, does not feel the need to compete. He does not need to look and see what others are doing or be "better than" the next person. Recognizing his capabilities for what they are, he strives *for excellence in his own life*. The only competition is with himself; to achieve greater personal growth.

RECOGNITION VS. PRAISE

PRAISE

Oh, how we love the sweet music of praise! Most people will go to almost any length to hear it. They will part with their money, work long hours, take physical or mental abuse, all for one word of approval. Just like the junkie who needs a "fix," they will go to any extreme to get "high." As they run from one "pusher" of praise to another, they become trapped in an addiction of approval. The more they are addicted, the more they abdicate their lives to others for direction.

Praise-seeking implies that you must constantly prove

your worth. Every time you make a mistake or do something you feel does not meet someone else's standards, you feel "less than" others. You then blame yourself and feel guilty for not doing what you think you "should." You keep on asking yourself, "Have I done well enough?" But the person who goes through life trying to do "well enough" develops the compulsive need to be or do "better than" others. And so one ill is piled on top of another. No matter how hard you try to be better than someone in any given area, you will feel inadequate because there are always those who, in your eyes, have surpassed you. They will have more money, larger homes, greater prestige, better physical attributes, etc. It is a game you can never win.

What, then, is there about praise which makes us act like flies around a sugar bowl? It is the replay of our childhood dependency when so much of our existence depended upon parental approval. Praise and blame were the means of control. If we were obedient and submissive, we were rewarded. If we resisted, we were punished. So deeply is the system of reward and punishment embedded in our subconscious minds and central nervous systems that we automatically respond to any form of praise or blame. Just as we spent a large portion of our childhood and adolescence in trying to please our parents, so, as adults, we will spend much of the remainder of our lives trying to please others.

The most destructive power of praise lies in its ability to make you identify with your actions. Praise says, in effect, that you are "good" because of your "good" acts and "bad" if you make a mistake or act "badly." Any time you do not meet the standards of the person praising you, you believe you have let them down and experience feelings of guilt. As a result, those who praise you can set you up so that they are in a position to control much of your life. As long as you serve their purposes, they will fulfill your need but when they want more from you than you are willing or able to give, they withhold the praise you seek and motivate you through guilt. They know that if they can make you feel guilty, you will do almost anything to regain their approval.

If you are to be totally free and self-confident, you must cease being caught in the trap of praise-seeking. To break this destructive habit, you must stop *placing others above yourself*. Never look up to anyone for any reason. If you do this you will never have to seek their approval and will no longer be seduced by praise or intimidated by blame.

RECOGNITION

There is a world of difference between praise and recognition. Recognition, as we shall use it here, is a factual observation. Neither a compliment nor a value-judgment, it is simply what the name implies: recognition that a person has done the best she or he can based on her or his present level of awareness.

The major difference between praise and recognition is that praise is a value-judgment. If you tell someone that he is a "great person" for doing something for you, you are also saying that he is "not such a great person" if he doesn't fulfill your desires. If your child brings you flowers, you shouldn't say, "You are a 'good boy' for bringing me flowers." If you do, you are implying that, if he doesn't bring them, he is a 'bad boy.' Instead say, "Thank you for the flowers. I appreciate them very much." This way you are giving the child recognition for his *action* without placing any value-judgment on him as a *person*.

Adults, young people and especially children respond much more to recognition than to the sweet talk of praise. They need to know that they occupy a special place in the lives of those around them. They want to be treated as persons, not non-persons; to be accepted for what they are, not what they "should" be. If they are given recognition for what they do based on their capabilities, they will sense that they are being acknowledged as individuals and not evaluated on the basis of their actions; that they are unique and worthy regardless of whether or not they measure up to other people's standards.

The difference between praise and recognition may be subtle but it is highly important in developing a positive self-confident personality. If people are not given the recognition they need to make them feel accepted as the truly unique individuals they are, they will resort to seeking praise and become its prisoner.

FREEING YOURSELF FROM OTHERS

We have already seen the high price we must pay for dependency and how our whole effort must be concentrated on trying to pry open the clenched grip each one of us has on the other. We are reluctant to lose the approval of family, friends, co-workers and peer groups by doing what we feel and know we should do. And so we let opportunity after opportunity pass by, afraid to pay the price of emancipation. *We could break away any time we wanted.* So, let's face it: the problem is ours.

Your fundamental responsibility, then, must always be your own physical and emotional well-being. By not breaking away, you are contributing to a situation of mutual dependency which imprisons those upon whom you rely as well as you. The fact is that, in the long run, they will get over their hurt or disappointment and, most importantly, if you meet your own needs first, will have new respect for you.

Nothing can stop you from achieving self-confidence, if you really want to. But until you free yourself from the mistaken certainty that dependency, manipulation, conformity, comparison and competition are essential to your well-being, you will not be able to function as an individual. Only when you decide that you are going to do everything you possibly can to free yourself on a mental, emotional, physical and spiritual level, will you be able to be the self-confident person you would like to be.

Bondage or liberty? The choice is up to you!

Secret #3
THE ART OF
SELF-ACCEPTANCE

Recognition of your own true worth as a person is another crucial factor in building self-confidence. Practically all your problems are the direct or indirect result of how you feel about yourself. It is a demonstrated fact of life that YOU CAN NEVER BE BETTER THAN YOUR OWN SELF-ESTEEM; that is, how you *feel* about yourself in relation to others, based on your sense of self-acceptance. These feelings are basically unconscious and have been programmed into your subconscious since early childhood.

Positive self-esteem is not the *intellectual* acceptance of one's talents or accomplishments. It is *personal* self-acceptance. Developing positive self-esteem is not an ego trip. You are not in love with yourself in an egotistical sense.

31

You simply realize that you are a truly unique and worthy individual; one who does not need to impress others with achievements or material possessions. In fact, the person who constantly brags and boasts has one of the classic symptoms of *negative* self-esteem.

On the surface, many people appear to have positive self-esteem. But this is not always the case. One of the tragedies of our time concerns those leaders, teachers, inventors, artists and people who have made great contributions to mankind and yet are victims of their own low self-esteem. Some of the most admired people in history have become drug addicts, alcoholics and even committed suicide just to escape from a self that they could never quite accept and often grew to hate.

Developing positive self-esteem is not just a matter of making yourself happy, it is the foundation on which you must build your whole life. If you can hope to be free, it is a task which you must take seriously. If you don't, you can only expect your low self-esteem to get even worse as you grow older until you end up like a tragic number of people who, at this moment, are sitting at home feeling sorry for themselves.

In order to compare the characteristics with your own behavior and personality pattern, it is important to know how low self-esteem is developed and how it manifests itself in others. You will then be able to see what you must do to improve yourself.

IN THE BEGINNING

There are three major causes of low self-esteem. The first is a series of self-defeating concepts, beliefs, and values that you have accepted from your parents. The second is a unique set of put-downs, received throughout your school years, from false and distorted concepts of teachers and such things as vocational placement analyses and IQ tests. The third stems from negative religious conditioning with its over-emphasis on feelings of guilt and unworthiness. While there are many other contributing factors to low self-esteem, these three are the most important. This chapter deals with the first of these.

By far the strongest single contributing factor to our faulty self-esteem is the low self-esteem of our parents. This is true especially of our mothers, the person with whom we usually spend our most impressionable years. Since most adults labor under false concepts, values and beliefs, these are passed on to children through attitudes, actions and reactions like a contageous disease. If parents feel, in any sense, inadequate and inferior, we, as children, feel unworthy and, as a result, are unable to cope with even the simplest problems in home or school life. In essence, our parents' "false" assumptions become the "facts" of our existence. The following will help you see why this happens.

When you were born, your brain was about one-eighth the size of an adult's. By eighteen months, it was about one-half adult size and, in five years, about five-sixth the size. It was the fastest growing organ in your body. *During this period of rapid growth, known as the "imprint period," your brain received those crucial permanent impressions which helped formulate your behavior pattern.* You can readily see that if one or both parents were suffering from low self-esteem at this time, how easily this might be absorbed by a child's impressionable mind.

It all started when you made your first mistake and were told you were a "bad girl" or a "bad boy." You misinterpreted this and felt that *you* were "bad" when, in reality, only your *actions* were "bad." The truth of the matter is that there is no such thing as a "bad child." The only thing "bad" about any child is the lack of *awareness* as to what produces the best results.

Obviously, there are certain things that a child should not do, things for which reasonable disciplinary action is necessary. But these, in themselves, never make the child "bad." By telling you that you were a "bad girl," or "bad boy" you identified with your actions rather than recognizing that *actions are but the means you choose to fulfill your dominant needs*, and that your choice, in some cases, was faulty and unacceptable. If a child is not made to understand this and believes that he is basically bad, he will develop feelings of unworthiness and inferiority which will be programmed into his subconscious mind. These feelings will subsequently manifest themselves as shame, self-condemnation, remorse and, worst of all, guilt.

A low or negative self-esteem is further developed through the common habit of belittling by comparison. When parents compare a child with a brother, sister or, particularly, someone outside the family, his own budding sense of inferiority is compounded. In the light of the flaws he has come to accept as part of his own make-up, he compares himself to children of the same age whom he admires. Believing that they are endowed with more strength, ability, popularity and self-confidence than himself, a devastating sense of inferiority overpowers him. If parents were to temper their criticism with encouraging phrases like, "You're far too nice a boy to let something like this happen," this kind of reaction could be largely prevented.

Lack of recognition or appreciation of individual uniqueness is another parental failing. Most parents pay little regard to their children's feelings, desires and opinions, rebuffing them with such maxims as, "Children should be seen and not heard!" and "Mother/Father knows best!" *They take disagreement as either a personal affront or out-and-out disrespect.* Leading analysts agree that this attitude is due to a low self-esteem which manifests itself in the need to always be *right*. These kinds of parents believe that their child alone has a problem but, actually, the problem is a mutual one involving both themselves and their offspring.

It is a disturbing fact that a large number of parents lead their lives vicariously through their children. Having decided that their offspring shall be everything they secretly yearned to be and are not, they push the child beyond his capacity. They want their own unrealized dreams of accomplishment to become reality. Of course, this is done at the child's expense. What such parents fail to recognize is that the child is unable to meet their unreasonably high standards simply because he or she has not developed—or may not even have—the emotional, mental, or physical capacity to do so.

Physical appearance, much more than is realized, is a major cause of low self-esteem. A number of children suffer from physical, mental and emotional handicaps because of unusual or abnormal physical appearance. By constantly bringing this to their attention and telling them that they are "too fat," "too tall," "too slow," etc., they develop deep feelings of inferiority which are difficult to overcome.

Some parents place high value on money and possessions. The child identifies with this and is imprisoned by a materialistic lifestyle which demands that he struggle and scheme. He or she often marries for money and pays a very high price for what they get. Frequently he is compelled, as the saying goes, to spend money he doesn't have, on things he doesn't need, to impress people he doesn't know. As materialism destroys the child's perception of his own true worth, he is committed to a life of chasing wealth to compensate for feelings of inferiority.

The previous chapter explains how most parents completely miss the mark when it comes to developing self-reliance in their offspring. Over-powering, over-permissive or over-possessive parents are usually the ones who turn their child into an emotional cripple. Deprived of the necessary motivation to face life situations with self-confidence and poise, he procrastinates and takes the path of least resistance. Lack of self-reliance fosters feelings of inadequacy and these, in turn, form the basis of low self-esteem.

Let's explore another pet premise of "there's-nothing-to-it" parenthood. Contrary to common belief, raising a child through a system based primarily on reward and punishment is guaranteed to perpetuate low self-esteem. The child must be permitted personal initiative and, without fear of punishment, allowed to make as many mistakes as necessary to learn his lessons. Once he has learned them, most likely, he will never have to repeat them. He will know that, whatever he does, he either earns his own reward or suffers the consequences of his mistakes. The earlier he realizes this, the better!

The most damaging aspect of interdependency is that we pass our low self-esteem from one generation to another. Research has tragically demonstrated that suicides follow along family lines. After what you have just read, this should not surprise you. It is easy to see that, if low self-esteem is inherited, in some cases the resulting manifestation will be extreme.

Besides contaminating our offspring with our inferiority, we tend to contaminate everyone with whom we come in contact. If we are in positions to influence others, such as teachers or clergy, we spread the disease to those who look to us for leadership and inspiration. They intuitively sense our lack of self-worth and inevitably begin to take on portions of what they identify and associate with us. I counsel hundreds of persons who have lacked the necessary self-confidence to meet life situations successfully. Each one of them was the product of the low self-esteem that was passed on to them from home, school and/or negative religious conditioning.

Low self-esteem has many manifestations or addictions. These can be described as the *means* and *habits* we develop to *escape* the demands of everyday living. They are simply alibis that permit us to temporarily avoid facing up to personal reality. The severity of the addiction we choose is in direct ratio to our sense of inadequacy and fear of having to justify who and what we are. The addicted person uses his alibi to cover up the low self-esteem he doesn't want others to see.

THE MAJOR ADDICTIONS
OF A PERSON
WITH LOW SELF-ESTEEM

BLAMING AND COMPLAINING:

We blame others and complain to and about them because we refuse to accept the fact that *we* are responsible for *everything* that happens to us! It is much easier to blame someone else than to say, "It is *I* who has the problem: or "It is *I* who must change." The person who habitually complains and blames others feels inadequate and tries to build himself up by putting other people down.

FAULT FINDING:

We find fault with others because they do not accept or comply with our own set of values. We compensate for our feelings of inadequacy by trying to make ourselves *right* and them *wrong*. Notice that we frequently do not like it when they do the things we most dislike about ourselves. When we find fault with their actions, in effect we are saying, "I don't like myself for doing that so I can't let you get away with it." It is psychologically true that we tend to dislike most in other people those faults or weaknesses of which we are most guilty.

NEED FOR ATTENTION AND APPROVAL:

Many people have a compulsive need for attention and approval. They are unable to recognize and appreciate themselves as worthy, adequate individuals of importance. They have a compulsive need for continuous confirmation that they are "OK," and that others accept and approve of them.

LACK OF CLOSE FRIENDS:

Persons with low self-esteem usually do not have close friends. Because they do not like themselves, they generally choose to be either "loners," living their lives apart from others, or manifest the opposite behavior pattern and become aggressive and overpowering, critical and demanding. Neither personality is conducive to friendship.

AGGRESSIVE NEED TO WIN:

If we have an obsession to win or be right all the time, we are suffering from a desperate need to prove ourselves to those around us. We try to do this through our achievements. Our motivation is always to receive acceptance and approval. The whole idea is to be, in some way, "better than" the next person.

OVERINDULGENCE:

People who "cannot live with themselves" because they do not like the way they are, usually try to satisfy their needs through a form of substitution. Feeling deprived and hurt, they seek mental and physical "opiates" to dull the ache. They overeat, take drugs, drink or smoke excessively to get temporary sensual satisfaction in order to cover up their emotional pain and desperate need for self-approval. Over-indulgence compensates for feelings of self-rejection. It gives them a temporary reprieve from facing reality and the growing need to change.

DEPRESSION:

We get depressed because we become totally discouraged with ourselves and our inability to accomplish the things we would like to do with our lives. We feel inadequate and unworthy because we have not achieved what we think we "should" or what others make us feel we "should" achieve. The frustration and anxiety in trying to live up to our own expectations and those of others cause us to have a severely low self-esteem.

DIVORCE:

Many divorces are the direct result of the low self-esteem of one or both partners. They generally occur in any relationship where one person has a compulsive need to control, dominate or possess the other. Excessive fault-finding results in bitterness and resentment, both of which are usually combined with a deep sense of inadequacy, insecurity and the desperate need to love and be loved.

GREED AND SELFISHNESS:

Persons who are greedy and selfish have an overwhelming sense of inadequacy. They are absorbed in their own needs and desires which they must fulfill at any cost to compensate for their lack of self-worth. They seldom have the time or interest to be concerned with others, even with the people who love them.

INDECISION AND PROCRASTINATION:

Low self-esteem is frequently accompanied by an abnormal fear of making mistakes. Afraid that he may not do what he "should" or what others *expect* him to do, he usually does nothing at all or, at least, delays doing anything for as long as possible. He is reluctant to make a decision because he feels that he is incapable of making the "right" one.

Another type of person in this category is the perfectionist. He has a similar personality only he always needs to be "right." Basically insecure, he is intent on being above criticism. In this way, he can feel "better than" those who, according to his criteria, are less perfect.

PUTTING UP A FALSE FRONT:

Those who put up a false front feel "less than" others around them. To counteract this, they often name-drop, boast or exhibit such nervous mannerisms as a loud voice or forced laughter, or use material possessions to impress others. They will not let anyone discover how they truly feel about themselves and, in an effort to hide their inferiority, put up false fronts to keep others—so they think—from seeing them as they really are.

SELF-PITY:

A feeling of self-pity or the "poor me" syndrome results from our inability to take charge of our lives. We have allowed ourselves to be placed at the mercy of people, circumstances and conditions and are always being pushed one way and then the other. We permit people to upset, hurt, criticize and make us angry because we have a leaning, dependent personality and like attention and sympathy. Many people accept sickness because there is great power in weakness. When we are sick, others give us the attention we desire and are motivated to do things for us.

SUICIDE:

This is the severest form of self-criticism. People who commit suicide are not trying to escape from the world, they are escaping from *themselves*; the self they have rejected and learned to despise. Instead of facing up to the condition which is at the root of their problem, they feel hurt and resentful and seek "to put an end to it all." Their problem, of course, is low self-esteem.

THE MOST COMMON EMOTIONAL, PHYSICAL AND PSYCHOLOGICAL CHARACTERISTICS OF A LOW SELF-ESTEEM

EMOTIONAL

Aggressive
Timid
False laughter
Boasting
Impatient
Tries to be "better than" others

Competitive
Arrogant
People Pleaser
Name Dropper
Critical
Rebels against authority

Perfectionist
Domineering
Dominates conversation
Procrastinator
Cannot admit mistakes
Compulsive drinker, smoker, talker, hobbiest

PHYSICAL

Sloppy appearance
Wilted handshake
Lackluster eyes

Grossly overweight
Turned-down mouth
Tense & nervous

Sagging posture
Weak voice
Can't look others in the eye

PSYCHOLOGICAL

Anxious
Vacillating
Dislikes, hates, rejects himself
Needs to be liked & accepted by everyone

Unsure
Thinks he is a loser
Ridden with shame, guilt, blame or remorse
Must be "right" all the time
Needs approval

Absorbed in own problems
Needs to win
Compulsive need for money, prestige or power
Does what others want him to do
Lives vicariously through his children, TV & hero worship

Now let's turn the illuminating glare of truth's spotlight on another area of your personality and consider the quality and structure of what is termed your AWARENESS.

Secret #4
THE PROBLEM OF AWARENESS

Because we are using familiar words to describe less familiar ideas, let's see if we can clarify things a bit, particularly where the techniques concern you, personally.

I don't care what you think you are. You may consider yourself exceptionally intelligent, overly stupid, underweight, overweight. You may be an activist or a pacifist, an office worker or an executive, a housewife or a career woman; an outgoing, friendly person or a timid wall flower. You may be an alcoholic, drug addict, liar, exaggerator, cheat or neurotic. You may be depressed all the time; fearful of everyone and everything. You may hate the weather, dogs, cats, exercise, bumble bees, traffic jams or spinach. But none of these really describes *you*. *They are only descriptions of the things you do or the actions you take*. If you *identify* solely with your *actions*, you are falsely perceiving the truth about yourself. You are judging, limiting, and even rejecting yourself without justification.

Poor self-confidence is simply a problem of *Awareness*. Once you are aware of the truth about yourself, you will be able to understand why you are the way you are and, most importantly, learn to love and accept yourself.

Your *Awareness* can be defined as the *clarity* with which you consciously and unconsciously perceive and understand everything that affects your life. It is the sum total of your life experiences, encompassing conditioning, knowledge, intellect, intuition, instincts and all that you perceive through your five senses. Your present level of Awareness indicates your moods, attitudes, emotional reactions, prejudices, habits, desires, anxieties, fears, aspirations and goals. Most important, it indicates your sense of personal worth; in other words, how you feel about yourself.

Awareness determines your concept of reality. Your mind is like a camera which is constantly taking pictures of the events in your life. You are the one who decides what kinds of scenes you wish to record on film and these things make up your Awareness. Your camera may record other people's negative characteristics or your own inadequacies, hopelessness or despair. You may read newspapers, watch TV or concentrate on other sources of dramatized tragedy, sickness or poverty, all of which are absorbed or mentally recorded. As you focus and file, focus and file, you eventually accept these things as reality because you have the pictures to prove it.

The problem is that truth and reality are not necessarily the same. If your mind has accepted false concepts, values and beliefs about yourself and others, your Awareness will be *faulty*. Although you will be operating from the wrong viewpoint, it will *seem* like the truth and you will take on the personality and behavior patterns to justify it. This all goes back to what we said in Chapter I.

Every decision you make and every action you take is based on your present level of awareness.

YOU ALWAYS DO YOUR BEST

Does this statement surprise you? Most people are shocked when they first hear it. You have been told for years that you can and should be better. And while this is basically good advice, if it is to be acted upon, it must be considered in the context of what constitutes your Awareness.

The fact is that you can never do better than you are doing at this moment because *you are limited by your present level of Awareness.* Even if your *best* is *faulty*, TO KNOW BETTER IS NOT SUFFICIENT TO DO BETTER. You will only "do better" when your Awareness is expanded.

ACCEPTING REALITY

It is imperative for you to recognize that you will be happy and at peace with yourself only to the degree you accept as reality the present frame of reference within which you are operating. Once you do, you will no longer be vulnerable to the adverse opinions of others. Conversely, if you don't like what others are doing because, in your eyes, it is not "right" or "fair," you have no justification for condemning and blaming them or making them feel guilty. The fact is that no one—either you or the other person—can do better than his or her best.

You must learn to accept the reality of the moment and realize that no other action is possible at the time.

Reality is the same for everyone. The difference between yours and someone else's is your perception and reaction to it. No two people have the same awareness. No two people have the same background and experiences and so their way of perceiving life—their values, concepts, beliefs, assumptions and aspirations—will be different.

The *personal reality* of each one of us consists of the mental, emotional and physical characteristics we cannot change *at this given moment*. Your personal reality, then, is the sum total of your present level of Awareness: the values, beliefs and concepts—right or wrong—you embrace right now. As perception is always colored and influenced by Awareness, if your Awareness is faulty so, too, is your perception even though you are sure you are right.

Every decision you make and every action you take is based on your present level of awareness.

Note well that practically all your emotional and most of your physical problems are the result of resisting *your own* or *someone else's* reality, or the reality of a *situation* that, at the moment, you are unable but desperately want to change. Your *refusal* or *inability* to accept things as *they are* is at the root of your problem. If you examine most of your disappointments and frustrations, you will clearly see that you are resisting something that cannot immediately be changed.

We resist reality, or "what is," because we are under the false and destructive assumption that we can change it. But things are the way they are whether we want to accept the fact or not. Only when we can *consciously* recognize a particular phase of reality for what it is *at the present moment* is our resistance to it overcome.

The key to change is to accept other people's behavior without feeling that you have "to set them right." You must allow them the personal freedom to live according to their own individual Awareness, however distorted and faulty it may be. To do this, you must learn to love and accept yourself first. If you are still judging yourself, you will feel compelled to judge others, thereby resisting their reality and present level of Awareness.

> *You can only be compassionate and understanding of others to the degree that you are compassionate and understanding of yourself.*

If you are not conscious that you are resisting reality, there is no way for you to break this destructive habit. You will always feel a need to judge things as "good" or "bad," "right" or "wrong," "fair" or "unfair." You believe that people and circumstances are conspiring against you because you can't face up to WHAT IS. And so you live in a world of wishful thinking where things "should be" but are not, a certain way.

It is a demonstrated fact of life that *what happens to you is not nearly as important as the degree of intensity with which you resist the reality of a particular situation or individual*. To put it another way, you can't help the way you feel about things, but you *can* help the way you think and react to them. You may not like the reality of a situation but you must accept it for the present moment. In so doing, you will have control over your responses.

One doesn't have to be a mental giant to see that resistance to reality is the cause of more heartache, headaches, resentment, hostility and family problems than anything else. You cannot possibly feel hurt emotionally, get angry, resentful or bitter towards another, nor can you ever feel "less than" or be "put down" and hurt by others without resisting reality.

THE DESTRUCTIVE POWER OF VALUE-JUDGING

The basic cause of most inharmonious human relationships is the tendency to impose our values on other people. We want them to live by what we have decided is "*right*," "*fair*," "*good*," "*bad*," etc. If they do not conform, we become resentful and angry, not recognizing that their level of Awareness makes them unable to comply.

By now, you must realize that there is nothing we can

do to alter other people's values, concepts or beliefs *if their Awareness is not ready to accept change*. No one is obligated to change just to make the world a better place for *you* to live in. People may disturb or anger you but the fact that not everyone objects to their behavior indicates that the problem is yours. You are resisting *their* reality and desiring to see things, not as they are, but as you would like them to be. This is the point at which you start value-judging.

Nothing can destroy a relationship or break off communications faster than value-judging.

If you wish to develop a positive self-esteem, it is imperative that you STOP ALL VALUE-JUDGING. This begins with the right motivation: the motivation that *all* forms of value-judging are disastrous to your well-being. Just discontinuing verbalized value-judgments is not sufficient. If you say one thing and think another, your words are meaningless for your thoughts are equally as powerful. The Scriptures remind us that, "As a man thinketh in his heart, so is he."

Motivation should encompass the knowledge that all value-judgments of *good and bad, right and wrong, fair and unfair* are totally unfounded because *everyone must inevitably do what they have to, whether it is correct or not. This is all their present Awareness will permit—no more, no less.*

Read this again! Let it become part of your Awareness. If you understand and believe this with the whole of your being, you will no longer feel the need to place value-judgments on yourself and others.

Simply to avoid value-judging because you have been

told that it is morally wrong will not change your behavior. Instead, you must cease value-judging yourself, then you will cease value-judging others, and start loving both yourself and others. When you learn to love and appreciate yourself, you will no longer be self-demanding and self-critical and will project this attitude to the outside world.

As soon as you start loving others as *they are*, the feeling will be reciprocal. Others will start loving you. They won't have any other choice. Think about it! Who are the people to whom you are most attracted? They are those you consider your close friends; the people who, no matter what they know about you, never pass value-judgments.

The secret of loving and being loved is to stop value-judging—forever!

UNDERSTANDING YOUR MOTIVATION

Perhaps *motivation* is one of the most misunderstood words in the English language. Executives often ask me to visit a company to "motivate" their employees. They are surprised when I reply that I cannot. All I can do, hopefully, is to inspire them to *change their Awareness*.

It is important for you to have a clear understanding of what *motivation* is. *Motivation describes your attitude when you would rather do one thing more than another at a particular time*. EVERYONE IS ALWAYS MOTIVATED. Whether you are actively seeking success in a certain field or are just plain lazy and prefer to sit in a chair, you are motivated. If you didn't want to lounge, you would do something else and that would become your motivation. The fact is that you can't start the slightest activity without first being motivated. What you must recognize is the difference between *positive* and *negative* motivation: the motivation to do something worthwhile and constructive and the motivation to do something which is destructive to your well-being.

In essence, no one can *be* motivated. Everyone is *self-motivated*. *YOU* WILL ALWAYS DO WHAT *YOU* WOULD RATHER DO THAN NOT. This generates your particular motivation.

Every action you take is a response to a personal need or desire that is determined by your present level of Awareness. Normally, your basic motivation is to feel good— mentally, physically, emotionally and spiritually. If your needs in any one of these areas are unfulfilled, they will create a sense of frustration and anxiety and you will do whatever you feel necessary to make yourself comfortable, even if that action is harmful to yourself.

HOW TO MOTIVATE YOURSELF POSITIVELY

If you want to have a more positive life experience, you must be convinced that any change you make *will bring about the gratification of a particular need or desire*.

Positive self-motivation begins with changing your Awareness. To make a constructive change in your life, you must evaluate the potential benefits for any given action. Then *you must convince yourself that the benefits will justify or outweigh the price you have to pay for them*. Others may inspire or even threaten you to make such a change, but it is *YOU* who must motivate yourself by means of 'profit and loss' comparison. To some degree, you have been doing this all your life only, now, you can make certain that the process will work *for* instead of *against* you.

The criminal, alcoholic, overeater or dope addict have all gone through the same process and, based on their levels of Awareness, decided that addiction is worth whatever price they have to pay for it. Once their Awareness changes— usually under tragic circumstances—they realize that the cost of *escaping* from reality and a self they have come to hate is too high for what they are receiving in return. And so their motivation sets them on a more positive course.

You will find it most helpful to cultivate the use of two familiar but often neglected words: "wise" and "unwise." All actions should be so classified. None should be labeled "good" or "bad," "fair" or "unfair," "right" or "wrong" because these are only moral judgments based on your present Awareness or the collective Awareness of society.

The terms "wise" and "unwise" do not impose value-judgments. They allow you to *observe* your actions or the actions of another and, on the basis of Awareness decide if they are "wise" or "unwise." At no time is *the person* being judged. Your actions may be faulty but you, *the person you really are*, must never be classified as "bad." This same understanding and courtesy must, in turn, be extended by you to everyone else.

I hope, by now, that you can see it is impossible to "motiviate" people to change by telling them what they "must," "should" or "ought" to do so. They can only change through their own *conscious decisions*. You may inspire, frighten or threaten them, but the motivation generated will only be temporary to fulfill their dominant need which, for that moment, is to get you off their backs. They will not change their habits permanently until they are convinced that the change will be beneficial to *them* in relation to the price they have to pay. What is more, they will not change until their Awareness is changed.

TAKING RESPONSIBILITY

You have the right and option to choose anything you want to do—*anything at all*. No one else can choose for you. Your Creator has given you *free will* to do *anything* you wish within the limits of your intellectual and physical capabilities. You are allowed to make mistakes, fail, lie, cheat, cry, shout, be lazy, angry, selfish, loyal, aggressive, rejected, hurt; to overindulge in food, drink or sex; to change your mind or do anything else you want. The Divine gift of individual choice is always yours, but free will certainly *does not* imply that you make the "right" choice all the time! Your choice is only as "right" as your present level of Awareness.

You have learned that, when you make any decision, it is based on a level of Awareness which is at a *fixed point* for that moment. You can do *one* thing and *only* one thing based on your current Awareness. Thus you are always doing the *best* you can under any present circumstances. You must give yourself the right to make mistakes, because it is through mistakes that your Awareness is expanded. Doing anything you want helps to release the emotional resistance and guilt which arise from the repression and unconscious programming of your subconscious mind.

You will never be free until you learn to be true to yourself and accept FULL RESPONSIBILITY for your own life and the fulfillment of your needs. But, in doing so, you must also accept FULL RESPONSIBILITY for every thought, word, deed and decision for, *inevitably*, you will have to pay the price for each. To use an old adage: if you want to dance, you must be prepared to pay the fiddler. You will learn and grow according to the nature and consequences of your actions.

Keep in mind that nothing you do is "right" or "wrong," "good" or "bad." It is only *wise* and *unwise*. As, hopefully, you progress from 'unwise' to 'wise' actions, the importance of this terminology will become increasingly evident.

Before you do anything, ask yourself the following questions:

Is this a wise or an unwise act?
Will it contribute to my basic needs?
Will it harm me or someone else?
Is it in harmony with Laws of the Universe as I understand them?
What is the *total* price I must pay?
Am I *willing* and *able* to pay this price and *accept the consequences*?

By asking these questions, you will put yourself in full conscious control of your life and affairs. They will help you to build a new Awareness based upon the knowledge that the person to whom you are accountable for all your action is YOU, yourself. The logic of this is quite evident when you consider that it is you who will reap the reward or suffer the consequences.

THE HOLD OF HABIT

Habits make you the person you are. It is impossible to make a major change in your life without destroying the compulsive hold they have upon you. Unless you are happy, healthy, calm, peaceful, self-reliant and successful in every area of your life, changing self-defeating habits must take priority in your life.

Most of us have no idea how much our lives are built around so-called "bad habits." We have programmed the wrong responses into our subconscious minds and central nervous systems. This causes us to respond the way we have conditioned ourselves to feel and act, no matter how negative, false, distorted or destructive this might be. Consequently, we must go through a period of unlearning or deprogramming in order to "decondition" ourselves.

YOU CANNOT GIVE UP ANYTHING YOU REGARD AS DESIRABLE.

No amount of will power is of any use unless we really want to give up old habits. Most of the time we want to get rid of their *painful effects* but are not willing to give up the habits themselves. The reason most diets fail after a short time is that the dieter starts feeling *deprived*. He has the desire to lose weight; to look and feel better. But he has *no desire to give up overeating* with the result that his mind is constantly filled with the thought of food. The more he thinks about food, the more conscious he becomes of it until the desire to eat consumes him.

We should not deceive ourselves that we can change our lives by self-discipline alone; by hoping that we can force ourselves to make a change. If a person really wants to lose weight, he must be "sold" on the idea of getting rid of the *habit of overeating* which has been serving as *compensation for tensions and unfulfilled needs*. He will seldom, if ever, stop simply because he thinks he *should*. To do this would only generate guilt, frustration and anxiety, all of which produce resistance to change.

Before you can change any habit, you must fully *recognize* and *accept* that you have one. *The fact that you can't accept your faults is the reason why you can't overcome them*. Verbally condemning your bad habits and yourself for having them only tightens their hold, thereby defeating all efforts to suppress them. Feeling guilty just makes the hold stronger. Alfred Adler put it this way. "Either do wrong

or feel guilty, don't do both. It's too much work." This is
a great piece of advice!

The Master Teacher warned us about the folly of putting
a patch of new material on an old garment, or pouring new
wine into old bottles. We must create new, more positive
habits by eliminating our negative habits through substitution; by providing worthy, positive thoughts and actions
to replace them. If your parents took something away from
you as a child, they usually offered you something else in
return. This kept your mind off what they had taken from
you.

There are some things we will give up readily. This is
because we have placed an importance on these things and
recognize their destructive effect on our lives. The more
importance you place on something, the more willing you
are to do something about it.

POSITIVE HABIT
CONDITIONING
PROGRAM

Use the following program to condition yourself to sub-
stitute any negative habit that you find detrimental to your
well-being.

STEP ONE

Write down the following:

A. What negative habit do you desire to replace?

B. What positive habit or attitude will you develop to replace it?

C. What *actions* will you take to replace your negative habit?

D. What is the easiest and most logical way to do this?

STEP TWO

A. Visualize yourself as already having succeeded in changing your habit. See yourself enjoying the benefits of your new positive habit.

B. Select and use a positive affirmation* to go along with the visualization.

STEP THREE

Observe your actions and note every time you fail to do what you promise. Remember, DO NOT condemn or scold yourself. Simply make a non-judgmental observation and allow yourself to make the necessary correction.

STEP FOUR

Keep a record for *at least* twenty-one days.

After you consciously choose your new positive habit pattern, these four steps will enable you to program it into your subconscious. It will then become an automatic reflex action.

---

*For example, I accept that I am a creator. Everything I can possibly be is right this moment part of my consciousness. I create exactly what I need.

If you have established negative responses to life situations, your automatic mechanism will cause you to respond the way you have conditioned yourself to FEEL and ACT. As it is necessary to keep a constant check on your responses or habit patterns, use the following three-step formula to check on and correct them.

1. Remove anything in your life that is not working for your good.
2. See what *is* working *right* for you and continue to program that into your subconscious.
3. Add new things you find desirable that are likely to work for you.

Keep up the above for the rest of your life and you will find that your life will be full of successful experiences. You can promise yourself anything but keep in mind that the important thing is to start using this program *right now*. If you do, you will begin to gain in self-confidence by knowing that you are doing something about changing your situation. The dynamic trigger action of keeping a promise for at least twenty-one days will work with attitude-strengthening magic.

Remember these important facts about changing your habits:

A. Recognize and accept the fact that you have a negative habit and place no value judgment on yourself;
B. Before starting to change your habit, weigh the

potential benefits against the price you will have
to pay for overcoming it;

C. No amount of will power is of any use unless you
really want to give up a habit;

D. You must be convinced that change will bring
about the gratification of a particular need or desire;

E. Above all, do not feel guilty, condemn or blame
yourself for your present condition. Up to now,
you have only done what your level of Awareness
has allowed.

William James observed that forming a new habit is like
winding a ball of string. The longer we can wind the string
without dropping the ball, the better off we are. If we drop
it and it rolls, we have that much more to wind again. As
a new habit becomes stronger, we are less and less tempted
by the old one. Even so we must remember that old habits
are never destroyed for good. They are only submerged.
For this reason, we must always be aware of our thoughts
and actions and keep *dominant thoughts* operating constructively upon new habits.

Secret #5
I'M NOT GUILTY, YOU'RE NOT GUILTY

Guilt is one of the most common forms of stress in our society. The world is full of guilt-ridden people. Unless you are one of those rare individuals who have overcome this destructive emotion, you probably share a variety of unnecessary guilt feelings with the vast majority.

Most of us have been *conditioned* to feel guilty. Family, friends, society, school, loved ones and religion have consciously or unconsciously turned us into guilt machines. We have been reminded since childhood of our so-called "bad behavior" and made to feel guilty about things we did or didn't do, or said or didn't say. Since most people are on a perpetual campaign to seek approval from others, they cannot handle guilt when it is imposed upon them from an outside source.

Guilt is the master tool of the manipulator. All a person has to do is to make us feel guilty and we are compelled to get back into their good graces as soon as possible. Most people can be manipulated into doing just about anything if they can be made to feel guilty enough.

Why do we permit this to happen to us? Simply because guilt has been associated with *caring* and, if you don't care, you are a "bad person." The truth is that guilt has nothing whatsoever to do with caring. Rather, it is a manifestation of neurotic behavior, behavior which, oddly enough, is accepted as "normal" by most people. In other words, to show that you really care, you are expected to exhibit a neurotic response. If you don't, you don't really care. This twisted line of reasoning controls the lives of a tragic number of individuals.

It is interesting to note that, in my classes, when I say one must never feel guilty, someone invariably raises his hand and asks, "Do you mean that I shouldn't *ever* feel guilty about *anything*?" Of course, what he is trying to say is that he has been so conditioned into feeling guilty that he feels guilty about not feeling guilty!

A LOOK AT MORALITY

A great many actions that are labeled "good" or "bad" by certain individuals, society or religious groups are nothing more than moral value-judgments based on *their* present levels of Awareness, which may be faulty. What is moral and right for you today at this point in your unfoldment, may not be moral and right for you tomorrow at another time or in another place. For morality varies from place to place and time to time.

Thomas Moore put it very well when he said,

> *I find the doctors and the sages*
> *Have differ'd in all climes and ages*
> *And two in fifty scarce agree*
> *On what is pure morality.*

Laws that are based on morality are not Universal Laws, for Universal Laws are immutable. They are few, simple and enforceable everywhere, always, automatically, without interference or moral value judgment by any group, religion or individual. There is no Universal Law to support guilt. Remember, GUILT IS A *LEARNED* EMOTIONAL RESPONSE.

THE SEVEN MAJOR FORMS OF GUILT

PARENT-CHILD GUILT

As a child, you were made to feel guilty by the adults around you and by your family in particular. After all, if they felt guilty, it was good for them so it must be good for you too! If they didn't like what you did or said, you were told that you were a "bad girl" or a "bad boy." A value-judgment was placed on *you* instead of your *actions*. Throughout your growing years, especially the first five, you were conditioned to respond to "good" and "bad," "right" and "wrong," with guilt being enforced through the reward and punishment system. It was at this time that you began to identify with your actions.

Parents unwittingly use guilt as a means of controlling their children. They tell a child that, if he doesn't do a certain thing, he will make them unhappy. Their weapons are phrases like, "What will the neighbors think?" "You embarrassed us!" "You disappointed us!" "You can do better!" "Where are your manners?" And the list goes on and on. Whenever you failed to please your parents, it was time for them to play the guilt game. As a result, you developed a behavior pattern of pleasing others first to avoid feeling guilty. You said what people wanted you to say and did what they wanted you to do, the ever-present inference being that, by conforming, everyone would like you. And so you developed the never-ending need to make a good impression.

CHILD-PARENT GUILT

In a reversal of the parent-child guilt game, children frequently use guilt to manipulate their parents. Most parents want to be "good" parents and cannot cope with the feeling that their child thinks they are unfair or don't love them. To coerce them, the child uses statements like, "You really don't love me!" or "So-and-so's parents let him do it." He also reminds them of the things they did or didn't do, things he intuitively knows will produce guilt feelings.

This behavior was learned by watching adults. The child doesn't know exactly how it works, only that it is most effective in getting what he wants. Since manipulation is the main concern in childhood, it doesn't take long for him to catch on.

Guilt is a *learned* emotional response. It is not *natural* behavior in a child. If your child is trying to coerce you through guilt, you can be sure he picked up the tactics from a good teacher—*YOU*!

GUILT THROUGH LOVE

"If you loved me..." are some of the most guilt-producing words used in a love relationship to manipulate the other partner. When we say, "If you loved me, you would do this," we are really saying, "Feel guilty if you don't do it!" or "If you refuse, you really don't *care* about me." Of course, we always must show that we care, even if it means taking on neurotic behavior! If words don't work, we can resort to such things as the silent treatment, refusal of sex, hurt feelings, anger, tears or tantrums.

Another tactic is using guilt to punish our partners for behavior which is inconsistent with our values and beliefs. Bringing up past transgressions and reminding them of how "wrong" they were helps stoke the flames of guilt. As long as our partners remain guilt-ridden, we can manipulate them. This type of relationship implies that our love is dependent on a particular kind of behavior we expect from our partners. When they do not conform, we use guilt to "set them right."

These are but a few of the ways to enforce guilt in a love relationship.

SOCIETY-INSPIRED GUILT

This starts in school when you fail to please your teacher. You are made to feel guilty about your behavior by being told that you could have done better or that you have let your teacher down. Without having to get to the root of the problem—the student's faulty Awareness—teacher-inspired guilt makes less work for the teacher and is an effective means of control.

Society tells you that you must conform. If you do or say anything that is not considered socially acceptable, you are made to feel guilty. Our prison system is an excellent example of the guilt theory in action. If you go against society's moral code, you are punished by confinement in an institution. During this time, you are supposed to feel guilty for what you have done. The worse the crime, the longer you have to feel guilty. You are then released, supposedly rehabilitated, without the real problem—your faulty Awareness, specifically your poor self-esteem—being corrected. It's no wonder that seventy-five percent of the inmates return to prison after commiting another crime.

Guilt feelings over social behavior condition you to worry about what others say or think of your actions. You become so concerned about their opinions that you are never free to do that which would mean self-fulfillment. Your primary concern is always to check with those around you before doing or saying anything which might displease someone. This is why etiquette is so strongly adhered to. To most people, it is a life and death matter which side of the plate to place the fork! Their whole lives are governed by socially-accepted behavior patterns because they cannot handle guilt. Unfortunately, people would rather be polite than be themselves.

SEXUAL GUILT

Sexual guilt has long been the American way of life. Past generations lived with sexual values which were inconsistent with natural desire. Enforced by religious conditioning where all forms of sexual expression were labeled either "good" or "bad," "natural" or "sinful," these were passed on from generation to generation like a contagious disease. If your value system included any form of sexual expression which was considered morally unacceptable, you were made to feel guilty and shameful. Things like masturbation, premarital sex, pornography, homosexuality, abortion and the like were all "bad" and "sinful." The result, today, is a variety of sexual hangups and taboos which produce repressed feelings of guilt.

Conditioned since childhood on the evils of sex, it is impossible for the average person to enjoy any form of sexual pleasure without a sense of guilt. Until he or she learns the valuable and basic lesson that *ANY FORM OF SEXUAL EXPRESSION WHICH IS WITHIN ONE'S OWN VALUE SYSTEM AND DOES NOT PHYSICALLY HARM ANOTHER PERSON IS RIGHT, REGARDLESS OF WHAT OTHERS SAY OR THINK*, he or she can never have a full and enriching sexual experience.

RELIGIOUS GUILT

Religion has done more than its share to develop and instill deep-seated guilt feelings in the average individual. Indeed, it may well take credit for the Original Sin of Guilt as guilt is the means by which it keeps its followers in line.

Through the mistaken interpretation of perfection, many religious denominations instill guilt in those who do not meet *their* moral value-judgments based on *their* interpretation of the Scriptures. They start with the premise that all judgment is based on perfection. Perfection, they say, is "good"; imperfection "bad." This mistaken interpretation has limited comprehension of the word's true meaning. If you put ten thousand of the same objects under a microscope, you would see that no two are exactly alike.

It is a biological, physiological, psychological and metaphysical fact that each entity is distinctly different. Each individual is an expression of Creative Intelligence. Perfection, and everything else for that matter, is relative. Wallace Stevens put it this way,

> *Twenty men crossing a bridge*
> *Into a village,*
> *Are twenty men crossing twenty bridges,*
> *Into twenty villages . . .*

Some churches, by expecting two people to perceive God, Truth and the Bible in the same way, have doomed their followers to failure.

Paradoxically, to be "perfect," you must have some flaws. Imperfections are the means by which you learn to grow; by which humankind is spurred on to create. To have no imperfections is to be sterile which is to have no need to develop mentally, physically, emotionally or spiritually. What is necessary to do "even greater works" is the desire to succeed which is untainted by guilt.

It is difficult for someone who has been programmed into believing that all sin is "bad" to see value and, yes, even beauty in sin and error. The church says that sin is "bad," yet few clergymen would deny that we learn from our mistakes. The difference may well be whether or not we learn the particular lesson they wish to teach us! Some of the world's outstanding achievements have come from individuals whose imperfections were the impetus to creative effort. If you read the biography of any great man or woman who has made a significant contribution to mankind, you will see, almost without exception, a person with flaws, many of which society has labeled "sinful." Being aware of this should enable you to put your own guilt into perspective. Guilt is totally unnecessary and self-destructive. Having the desire to overcome so-called "imperfections, sins and mistakes" is sufficient.

SELF-IMPOSED GUILT

The most destructive form of guilt is that which is self-imposed. This is guilt we impose on ourselves when we feel that we have broken our own moral code or the moral code of society. It originates when we look at our past behavior and see that we have made an unwise choice of action. We examine what we did—whether it was criticizing others, stealing, cheating, lying, exaggerating, breaking religious rules or committing any other act we feel is wrong—in the light of *our present value system*. In most cases, the guilt we feel is an attempt to show that we care and are sorry for our actions. We are, at once, whipping ourselves for what we did and attempting to change history. What we fail to realize is that the past cannot be changed.

The neurotic always feels guilty. The balanced, wholesome personality *learns from the past*. There is a world of difference between the two.

Going through a self-inflicted guilt sentence is a neurotic

trip you must stop if you are ever to develop a self-confident personality. Feeling guilty won't help you one iota. It will only keep you a prisoner of the past and immobilize you so that you cannot take any positive action in the present. By harboring guilt, you *are escaping the responsibility of getting on with the business of living.*

GUILT ALWAYS BRINGS PUNISHMENT

Guilt always brings punishment. Punishment may take many forms: depression, feelings of inadequacy, lack of self-confidence, poor self-esteem, an assortment of physical disorders and the inability to love yourself and others. Those who cannot forgive others and hold resentment in their hearts are the same people who have never learned to forgive themselves. They are the guilt-ridden people.

Trying to ignore your mistakes is just as damaging as holding on to the guilt they have caused you. Mistakes should be treated like a speck of dust in the eye. As soon as you identify the problem, don't condemn yourself or feel guilty for having it. Just get rid of it. The sooner you do, the sooner you will be free from the pain it is causing you. Only then will you be able to live a creative life and begin to express your unlimited potential.

LEARNING FROM THE PAST

Learning from past behavior is important to developing a wholesome personality. But *feeling guilty about what you have done is not learning from the past*. Learning from the past means recognizing mistakes and resolving, to the best of your ability and Awareness, not to repeat them. Mentally whipping yourself over what you have done or wasting valuable time and energy on feeling guilty, remorseful, shameful or unworthy is not part of this lesson. Such negative emotions only prevent you from changing your present situation because your dominant attention is focused on the past.

Nobody can live in the past and function creatively in the present. Your mind cannot cope with two realities at the same time and reflects whatever occupies your dominant attention. If you are giving your dominant attention to what you have or should have said and done, the present will be one of frustration, anxiety and confusion. This is much too high a price to pay. It is far better to forgive yourself and, with a positive and happy attitude, move on towards the future.

REMEMBER— YOU ALWAYS DO YOUR BEST

You always do your best. Mark it well and don't forget it! Every decision you make and every action you take is based on your level of *Awareness at that moment*. You can never be "better than" your present Awareness, for it is the clarity with which you perceive any situation. If your Awareness is faulty, you will have a faulty experience which may cause you to do or say things you will regret later on. Because your Awareness is fixed at a certain level, whatever you did or didn't do, whatever you said or didn't say, was your best, even if your best was faulty or unwise. The simple fact is that *you had only one choice and that was governed by your Awareness at that moment*.

YOU ARE NOT YOUR ACTIONS

You are not your actions. Your actions are only the *means* you use to fulfill your dominant needs. They may be *wise* or *unwise* but this does not classify you as "good" or "bad." At the very source of your being, you are a perfect individual who, for the moment, may be acting upon a faulty Awareness. The Scriptures state clearly that you are made in the image and likeness of God. If this is true, then you must already be perfect but are prevented from this realization by your existing Awareness. The more you accept the Biblical Truth, the more you will be able to express that perfection. Remember, God doesn't turn out faulty products!

MAKE A GUILT DIARY

Here is a personal experiment you will find interesting and helpful. For the next twenty-one days keep a guilt diary. Observe yourself in action for this three-week period. Make copious notes and record all the details—

1. Every time you try to make someone else feel guilty.
2. Every time someone tries to make you feel guilty.
3. Every time you try to make yourself feel guilty.

By doing this, you will become acutely aware of how much time is spent playing the guilt game. Every time you try to make yourself or someone else feel guilty, stop right then and there. This will change your habit patterns until, soon, you will cease playing the game altogether.

Every time you sense someone is trying to make you feel guilty, let them know that their game is no longer effective. *The victim must let the exploiter know that he is no longer vulnerable.* At first, they won't believe you because they have been manipulating you for so long, but once they realize that you no longer need their approval, they will cease trying to make you feel guilty. Remember, the *only* thing you owe them is your honesty.

Secret #6
THE POSITIVE POWER OF LOVE

Love has inspired books, songs, works of art, great achievements and even the course of history. It is the bond that holds humankind together.

There are many definitions of love, yet each one is inadequate. We have definitions from Charlie Brown, Webster's Dictionary, Eric Fromm and even the Bible. Love can be found in the dictionary somewhere between 'like' and 'lust.' And maybe that's where it belongs!

To understand what love *is*, we have to understand what love is *not*. Love is not hate, violence, ambition or competition. It is not infatuation. Infatuation focuses only on external traits and is merely a form of conquest. It's a neurotic state which fills a personal need so that conquest is invariably followed by disappointment.

Take the neurotic woman. She marries a man because he is handsome, then says that all he thinks about is his looks. She marries him because he is intelligent, then feels stupid and accuses him of knowing it all. She marries him because he is steady and sensible, then finds him boring and dull. She marries him for his money, then is disgusted because all he thinks about is business. She marries him because he is sexy, then objects when he is sexually attractive to other women. And on and on it goes!

Love is not sex. You can have sex without love, and love without sex. The sexist attitude of society has placed labels on women which must be overcome if a woman is to be treated as a person and not as a sex object. But leaving labels aside, when sex and love are combined, the result is a beautiful, spiritual experience, one unequalled by any other.

What, then, is love? *Love is the attracting, uniting, harmonizing Force of the Universe*. Love is wanting to be with one person more than any other and wanting to support that person in all that they can be. It's helping her or him grow emotionally, mentally, and spirituality. Most of all, love is allowing another person the complete freedom to be himself or herself and accepting that person without trying to change him or her. If these concepts are to work, they must be adhered to by both parties. The trouble with many relationships is that love is one-sided.

In order for a relationship to be balanced, you must give, but also expect to receive. Your needs must be met as well as those of your partner. The compulsion to keep giving without expecting a return, or keep receiving without expecting to give is the sign of a neurotic personality. To love means to love *period*. It doesn't mean, I will love you if...until...or when. There is no emotional blackmail. This is the positive power of love.

A child's ability to love is usually set by the time he or she is thirty-six months old. This is why it is important to build the child's self-esteem right from the beginning. The key here is showing the child that he is accepted for what he is, teaching him that this attitude should be reciprocal and, as a parent, being an adequate role model.

If a young woman has poor self-esteem, she will often marry the first man who comes along, fearing that her opportunities are limited. Sensing her inferiority, the man will play on her feeling of inadequacy and try to dominate her. Since she really does not like herself, she, in turn, will be constantly seeking approval and the love she didn't get as a child. The odds are that she will end up either in the divorce courts or with a husband who is an alcoholic, neurotic, psychotic or, perhaps, something worse. If self-confidence, self-acceptance and the acceptance of others had been cultivated early in life, most of these pitfalls would have been avoided.

It is important in a relationship to *preserve* love. In order to do this, it is necessary to realize that you are not a *couple* or *twosome* or anything else. Despite the abundance of poetic imagery, it is literally impossible to merge two human beings as one. You are simply separate *individuals* who have found a great deal to share together. You came into the world alone and you will leave this world alone.

The thrills of ardent romance notwithstanding, it is sheer folly to promise to love another person forever! While it is beautiful to hear someone so declare, it is an empty promise. Think about it for a moment. You cannot count on your lover loving you forever, no matter what he or she says, for love is a moment-by-moment experience. Yesterday's love has been spent, tomorrow's love is not here yet, and today's love must be earned. The fact is that *love will only continue as long as each person contributes to the relationship*. And love must continue if a relationship is to be held together. A legal contract won't do it!

Preserving love depends on a totally free relationship. One individual must not attempt to *change* the other. This happens much too often and is a major contributing factor to break-up and divorce.

Love, romance and excitement are all possible when you permit your partner to express his or her own individuality. If a relationship is not stifled by unreasonable demands and expectations, it will actually grow closer. The more independent you feel, the more you will value your partner. True love depends on true freedom. Only those who are free can afford to love without reservation.

Time spent together should be devoted to motives of love and sharing those things you both enjoy. This will eliminate boredom and keep the relationship alive. Vital, in this regard, is the development of a romantic personality.

There are those who feel that romance does not last forever; that it is normal for the initial glow to fade and a more 'mature' relationship to develop. If you wish to accept this, fine. But, in so doing, you are cheating yourself out of one of life's most beautiful experiences. A 'mature relationship' is just another way of saying that a couple has made an uneasy compromise to maintain a *tolerant* status quo.

Without romance, a person's life lacks magnetism, so it is important for you to cultivate it. A romantic personality will increase your magnetism and enable you to attract the people, events and circumstances you desire. We all need romance in our lives and are grateful to those who stimulate and encourage it. King Solomon fell in love a thousand times. He was known as the wisest man on earth! A romantic person is a *wise* person.

Everyone wants to be loved. Every stranger you meet is crying out inside, "Please love me." Sometimes this is difficult to justify in the light of our actions; sometimes the individuals, themselves, don't recognize this as the inner hunger they feel.

Most people believe that they are not loved enough. This is because they cannot recapture the love they once knew as children. If they were fortunate, this was mother-love; love in its most perfect form. And so they go through life trying to regain this perfect emotion by searching *outside* of themselves.

Look at your life! You go to the grocery store for food, to classes for education, to the doctor to get well, to a contractor to build your house, to the beauty parlor to have your hair done, to the department store for your clothes. And so it is with love. You go to others for love. Like a carrot dangled before a horse, there is love, just out of reach!

STOP LOOKING FOR OTHERS TO LOVE YOU

If you are seeking someone to love you as the launching point of your love program, you will go through life disappointed. Love begins with loving yourself and being yourself. It has to *start* with you. Unless you first love yourself, you will not be able to find it in another. Only when you generate love and radiate it forth until it embraces everything and everyone, will love be yours in return.

But remember, you cannot *give* your love to another person. You can only be *loving*. Being loving means learning to love your mind, thoughts, body, life and the God-power within you. Learn to love objects like trees, flowers, animals, sunshine and everything you see, touch and taste. Have you ever noticed how some people always have trouble with their automobiles? Their vehicles just don't respond to them. Yet another person "talks" to his and it responds trouble-free, trip after trip. It would seem that even inanimate things can sense love. Preposterous? It has been scientifically demonstrated that metal atoms respond differently to different personalities.

Loving is one of our strongest needs. It has been discovered by behavioral scientists that it is not *lack of love* which causes negative personality disorders but *lack of loving*. One man proved this while running a ranch home for delinquent boys and girls. Upon entering the home, the children were given an animal to feed, care for and learn to love. For many of them this was the first form of life they could love. The success rate in rehabilitation was outstanding.

DOING UNTO OTHERS

The idea that we cannot possibly love another until we have first learned to love ourselves may, on the surface, appear to be a very self-centered philosophy. But it isn't if we realize that we are in consciousness with every other person on earth. In the same way that our heads are joined to our shoulders, our hands to our arms, our feet to our ankles, each person is an extension of everyone else. An infection in one part of the human body means that the entire body is affected; to hurt another person mentally, physically or emotionally, means that we are hurting ourselves.

For this reason, we cannot say, "To hell with the rest of the world, I'm going to take care of myself." Instead, by first loving ourselves, we make it our personal responsibility to elevate the consciousness of humankind for, like a chain, the human race is only as strong as its weakest link.

SOME IMPORTANT ASPECTS OF LOVE AND THEIR RELATIONSHIP TO YOUR INDIVIDUAL PROGRESS

Remain calm and love regardless of the circumstances. Love is not a placid state but a conquering force. If someone does something to you which seems unjust or unfair, learn to forgive that person, for forgiveness is part of love. Mentally note that the situation has come into your life as a lesson. The way you meet the experience will determine whether or not you understand the meaning of love. If you do, you will be able to forgive knowing that everything will work out for the good of all concerned. To pass 'love lessons' victoriously is to reach new dimensions of success, prosperity, peace and fulfillment.

Learn to love everything that happens to you because your experiences give you a chance to grow in the consciousness of love. Say to yourself many times a day, "I am growing in the consciousness of love." If you succeed, the truth of everything with its ten-fold return will enrich your life in marvelous ways.

Many people go through life hating, criticizing and condemning others for their own lack of love. These are the negative people. They have a talent for putting others down with joking sarcasm and making them feel so inadequate and useless that they either hold back, withdraw or just plain give up. Negative people withhold love, recognition and compliments because they must always say what is on their minds, regardless of how destructive it is. They justify their verbal hostility as "constructive criticism," an "honest relationship" or even "objective appraisal." Their greatest talent lies in the ability to find and identify the weaknesses in others instead of their strengths.

In New York a few years ago, I conducted a seminar for married couples. One of the projects was for each person to list ten good things about his or her mate. I offered a prize for the first one finished. What was interesting but not surprising about this experiment was that, by the time the first one had finished, some had not even put down *one* item. These people were either unwilling or unable to write one positive or complimentary characteristic about the person with whom they were sharing their life.

It is common knowledge that, when plants are praised and spoken to positively, they thrive and grow, but when they are condemned and rejected, they become stunted or even die. If you have this effect on your plants, just think of the effect you have on another human being!

The Positive Power of Love determines how successful you will be in life. In order to be successful, you must be able to get things done. There are three ways of doing this: to do the task yourself, get someone to help you, or team up with others and *give* help.

The first method is the most common, but it is also the most limiting because you are restricted to the amount of time and effort you, personally, can expend. If you read the biographies of great achievers, you will notice that they generally become successful by expanding their growth through the efforts of others. In other words, they get things done by either receiving or giving help.

Giving help is one of the little known secrets of success. You get things done by helping others get things done. If you are a supervisor, manager or boss, by assisting those under you to become successful, you become more successful yourself. If you are a teacher, success comes in direct proportion to your success with students; it comes by showing them how they can get what *they* want, not what *you* want. Any relationship, including marriage, will only grow when you learn to give others a helping hand.

Love is the means by which you help others to be successful. It expresses itself in the ability to make others feel important, alive and capable of self-improvement. By giving others recognition and assurance, and pointing out their positive traits, you will stimulate them to make the best possible use of their unlimited potential. The most you can do for other people is to open their eyes to their own greatness; to the potential they never realized existed. This is what "loving thy neighbor" is all about.

But helping others is not a one-way street. By offering encouragement and pointing out people's strengths, you are helping yourself as well. Not only will you satisfy your own need to be loving, each positive action will generate an even more positive response and increase your total self-confidence.

Emmet Fox put it so well when he said, "Sufficient realization of love will overcome anything. There is no difficulty that love cannot conquer, no disease it will not heal, no door it will not open, no guilt it will not bridge, no wall it will not tear down, no sin it will not redeem. Love will lift you to the highest dimension." And that is where you must be.

I love everything I do. I love my work. I love traveling. I love my audiences. And I love writing this book for you!

Secret #7
MIND, YOUR OWN BUSINESS

Scientists recently commented that the next great area to be explored by man should be the space between his ears. To this day, relatively little is known about the human mind and its principal tool, the brain.

Like electricity, the mind is a usable force which has existed and will continue to exist for eternity. Its powers stagger the imagination. While, every day, science is learning more and more about its tremendous potential, we should not—must not—wait for a blueprint to make full use of that with which we are naturally endowed.

The longer you wait, the more you study and research elsewhere, the further away you will get from whatever it is you are searching for. You need not look beyond that

which is *within* for the self-confidence and power to solve
all your problems and make life as you wish it to be. The
Power which created and sustained you did not put you
together so that you would have to read a book, take a
course, or wait for a scientific breakthrough to experience
life to its fullest potential. From the beginning, the answers
have been within you. You have always possessed the wisdom, intuition and mental resources to express life fully and
perfectly.

Everywhere people are searching, praying, looking,
struggling and striving for self-confidence, spiritual development and the material things they desire, unaware that
no one or no thing outside themselves can help. Their families can't, their friends can't, their bosses can't, the government can't, even religion can't. The reason for this is
simple, so simple that it escapes the majority of humankind.
As the Master Teacher reminded his followers, *"Everything
you need is right within you."* Although he repeatedly said,
"Lo, do not look here, do not look there, the Kingdom of
Heaven is *within you,*" millions of people still haven't gotten
the message that they are personally endowed with the ability to choose and the potential power to accomplish anything
they desire.

Education, government and religion have combined to
create a subtle atmosphere of dependency that places and
keeps the average individual in a state of mental bondage.
As a result, most people look outside for help. They want
everyone, God especially, to do for them what they should
be doing for themselves. They are unaware that all the
wisdom, intuition, perfection, love and ability they need
resides within them and that these great powers are waiting
to be released.

YOU, INCORPORATED

For the purpose of our study, we shall break down the three primary *phases* of Mind into Conscious, Subconscious and Superconscious. Throughout this explanation, you must remember that you do not have three minds. You have only *one* with three phases. It's just like the air. There is not my air and your air. There is only universally present air and we all use a portion of it. So it is with the mind. Your mind is that portion of the one universal Mind which you are using and it is broken down into three phases. The boundaries cannot be clearly defined so that the labels tend to be far more precise than the phases they represent.

The business of living a creative life and achieving total self-confidence requires that you get on a first-name basis with the three phases of your mind and understand the primary functions of each. I call this joint venture of all the phases working together YOU, INCORPORATED.

Everything that is happening to you emotionally, mentally, physically and spiritually is the unfolding of what is happening in your mind, that tremendous electrical power which is able to reproduce accurately all the feelings, thoughts, sensations, sights, sounds and stimuli from the outside world. Think about your eyes and how they work in amazing coordination with your brain to enable you to see. You do not really see with your eyes, but with your brain! As a principal tool of the mind, the brain can picture and project the vibratory pattern of anything you wish. Its electrical pulsations are forms of energy which have the power to create in the outer world anything you accurately picture in the inner world of your mind. By controlling your mind, you control your life!

As a result of splitting the atom, scientists discovered that a tremendous power can be produced when we are able to tap invisible wave lengths of energy in the universe. Mohammad talked about this power when he said, "Split an atom and in its heart you will find a sun." Your mind is really a tremendous, atom-splitting cyclotron, able to release a stream of dynamic creative energy which will form whatever you picture and imprint upon invisible substance and make it an outer reality. An idea held in the mind has the ability to attract to itself all the elements it requires to bring forth whatever you desire.

While sending rockets into the illimitable void of time and space, vast electro-magnetic forces have been discovered in the universe. These forces work under the laws of attraction and repulsion, the same laws that control the gravity of the earth, sun and stars. A similar electromagnetic force exists in your mind with your blood, a principally saline solution, being the greatest conductor of electricity. Just think about the Intelligence that devised the amazing system whereby nerve currents from the brain are transmitted to all parts of the body instantaneously. This same Intelligence works through your mind to produce that which you picture and hold there.

Electricity is magnetic. The world is full of electricity. So is your body. You must build a constant Awareness to this fact and learn to generate your magnetism to attract, not repel, the things you desire in life.

THE LAW OF MENTAL MAGNETISM

The Law of Mental Magnetism states that *you will draw to yourself that which you most persistently think about*. And, here, we must remind ourselves of something we said earlier: no person is what he thinks he is, but what he *thinks*, he is!

The Law of Mental Magnetism is similar to nature's law of magnetism. Let me give you an example. If you were to take an iron magnet, it would draw any iron substance to it. But it would attract *only* iron and reject all other materials. LIKE ATTRACTS LIKE. Why is a magnet a magnet? Simply because all the molecules are pointed in the same direction. Their pulling power is *fused* together. Ordinary metal molecules are pushing and pulling against each other. Implicit in this phenomenon is the value of unity of purpose.

Whatever you give *dominant thought* to, whether it be sickness or health, success or failure, abundance or lack, love or hate, the object of your attention will be attracted to you. Your brain cells are sending out magnetic thought waves which can travel to infinity. Each cell is a *want* cell and it combines with others to attract *the sum total of your wants*, whether they be negative or positive.

The important thing is to *know* exactly *what you want*. If you don't you will attract only confusion. You may say, "I don't *want* sickness, yet I am sick." But what are you most persistently thinking about? What are you giving your dominant attention? Sickness!

Ernest Holmes, a noted teacher and metaphysician, was approached by a friend suffering from a severe cold. He asked Holmes to treat his ailment. Ernest's response was, "Your cold seems to be doing all right for itself. Let's treat you for your health!" Remember, LIKE ATTRACTS LIKE. The law always works.

People who are not clear on what they really want consistently attract things which seem inconsistent with their wishes. Everybody, on the surface, wishes for such things as success, friendship, love, happiness, safety and security, but due to erroneous thinking processes, these are not what they subconsciously *want*. One out of ten thousand really understands this amazing fact.

If you ask people to list their most important wants, you will notice something strikingly similar about their lists. The items have one thing in common: *they are all positive*. This is because we only admit to ourselves and others those things of a positive nature. No one ever says that he wants to fail, be sick, poor, unhappy, or insecure. Everyone claims just the opposite. But here is an amazing fact: like the magnet with its opposite attracting and repelling poles, for every POSITIVE WANT, we have a NEGATIVE want WHICH WE WILL NOT ADMIT and which, often, we are not even aware exists. Thus it is imperative to know *exactly what we desire* for The Law of Mental Magnetism always attracts our true wants. It does not attract our wishes, whims or passing fancies.

Everyone says they want success but the truth is that they really don't want it at all. They don't want to do the things which make up a successful personality. People aren't successful because they have money. They have money because they are successful. Most of us want the *results* of success but not the responsibility that goes along with it. With all the knowledge, education and training available today, it's harder to fail than succeed. But success scares most people and so they fail because, subconsciously, they want to.

There are those who say they want friendship or love yet criticism, hate, jealousy, envy and revenge dominate their attention. There are those who say they want popularity and recognition but, at the same time, make their desire for privacy obvious. There are those who say they want happiness, yet go about being depressed, angry, rejected, resentful and self-pitying. And the list goes on and on. The simple fact is that you will give your dominant attention to what you really want, and what you give your dominant attention to will be yours through the Law of Mental Magnetism.

The Law of Mental Magnetism also applies to the radiation of your thoughts. If you throw a pebble into a pond, you will see ripples going out in circles. These circles ultimately reach the shore. If you were to take two stones of different sizes and weights and toss them both in at the same time a few feet apart, their ripples would eventually converge. In the ensuing struggle for supremacy, the larger ripples from the larger stone would overcome the smaller ripples from the smaller stone. So it is with your thoughts. The larger the thought, the bigger your thinking, and the bigger your thinking, the more easily it will vanquish smaller thoughts. Positive thoughts set up waves which are bigger, more energetic and have stronger vibrations. These more powerful vibrations reach their objective because, like the big stone in the water, they create higher and stronger waves.

Science can now measure thought waves. In tests, subjects are able to think about a certain object and project the thought wave until it is picked up and measured by a photographic apparatus. If the subject, for example, were to concentrate on an object such as a triangle, the apparatus would produce a perfect picture of the triangle.

Other successful experiments involve photographs taken of ordinary drinking water while it is being prayed over and blessed. Preliminary photographs of the water showed very thin vibrations but as the same water was being sanctified, it registered significantly increased radiation indicating that the power of positive thought can be transferred to an object.

Every time you send out a negative thought, just like turning off the electric light switch, you automatically *lower* the magnetism in your body and mind. Thoughts of sickness, poverty, hate, resentment, lack and limitation disconnect you from your creative power to magnetize and attract. The more this happens, the more you run down your mental power source until, like an automobile battery which has been drained, it finally dies. Fortunately, you can recharge your battery and become an increasingly magnetic individual by using positive thoughts and words. Remember, positive creates; negative destroys.

It is time, then, that we begin to learn how our mind operates and how we can use the correct thinking process to magnetize and attract the good things we want in our life experience. In this chapter, we shall become familiar with the first of the three phases of mind power: the superconscious.

THE SUPERCONSCIOUS PHASE OF MIND POWER

The Creative Mind has been called various things by philosophers, psychologists and mystics throughout the ages. An ancient and interesting example of its use involves Moses who heard a voice speak to him from a flaming bush. When he willingly responded, he was given the Ten Commandments and shown how to lead the Lost Tribes out of the desert to freedom. Asked who had directed him, he replied, "I AM has sent me." Undoubtedly, he was referring to the Creative Intelligence in every human being.

The experience of Moses demonstrates that, within each one of us, is a power center which *knows the perfect way* for us; a realm of Absolute Ideas that *cannot be wrong*. This source, which we can contact at will, always gives us the information we need to lead us out of barren places into more productive fields. William James called this transcendental power the Superconscious Mind. Emerson referred to it as the Universal Mind. Whatever you call it, just believe that it *does* exist and, because it always knows the perfect way for you, that you can tap its unlimited potential to receive the creative ideas you need to solve your problems.

GREAT PEOPLE HAVE USED THIS POWER

You can build self-confidence by releasing your unlimited potential through the power of your mind. Just as an artist forms a picture *first* in his mind, the law of magnetic attraction can bring you that which you picture in detail. Clara Barton used this power. She pictured helping people in distress and, from this, emerged the Red Cross. Betsy Ross pictured how she would make the American flag and her mental picture became a reality. Joan of Arc heard voices guiding her as the Creative Mind led her to victory.

The Bible speaks of this power within which knows all. The Master Teacher referred to it simply, dramatically, when he said, "It is not I, but the *Father within*; he doeth the works."

The philosopher Epictetus put it this way:

> *When you have shut your doors, and darkened your room remember never to say that you are alone, for you are not alone; but God is within, and your genius is within . . . and what need have they of light to see what you are doing?*

Most people believe that there is a Higher Power that controls and brings order to the universe. The conception of this Higher Power differs from individual to individual and from group to group, but most will agree that it does exist. If you have gotten that far, then you must ultimately arrive at the conclusion that there is some way in which this

Power can communicate with us and we can communicate with it, just as all great teachers and thinkers have done. We make contact through the Superconscious phase of Mind and we do this when we meditate.

It is vitally important that we regularly take time from our busy schedules to become still and allow the Superconscious to speak and guide us. It does not speak to us in English, French, Italian or any other language, it speaks to us through *intuition* which manifests itself as a *feeling* or *desire*. When we receive intuitive feelings from the Superconscious, we are guided to the people, places or circumstances we need to fulfill our creative purpose.

We can readily see this intuitive power expressing itself in the animal kingdom. Watch a bird build a nest. No one has taught it how to build one. It relies solely on intuitive guidance which shows it how to construct the nest perfectly. In the animal kingdom, we call this instinct; in humans, it is called intuition. This same guided intuition channeled through our minds will show us how to construct our lives perfectly once we become open and receptive to it.

Remember that the Superconscious phase of mind is the realm of *absolute ideas*. It knows the perfect way so it *can never be wrong*. When we learn to trust it, we will make fewer mistakes because we will be guided by *Infinite Wisdom*. This is the Source of wisdom that has guided all the great minds.

CREATIVE POWER CHANNELED THROUGH DESIRE

Creative Intelligence channels its Creative Power through *desire*. Our entire world was built on the magnetic thoughts of those who had a *desire* to create, move forward, and lead humankind. *Desire is the seed of fulfillment. Whatever your mind can conceive, believe and picture MUST become a reality for you.*

Creative Intelligence speaks to you through intuition. This intuition manifests itself as a *desire* to do something creative. Desire works its magic through the power of the sympathetic nervous system. When you want something strongly enough, the desire becomes imprinted upon your subconscious mind. The emotion is then transmitted to the nerves and muscles of your body and you are impelled to achieve it.

The most important thing to remember about desire is that if you have the desire to do *anything* creative, you also have within you the *means* of fulfillment. Creative Intelligence would not have given you the desire if that potential were not *real* for you. In other words, whatever desire you have, no matter how far-fetched it may seem, carries with it the ability and mechanics to make it become reality. Every person who has accomplished something worthwhile started out with a *desire*. At its inception, to most of these people the realization of this desire seemed remote, but faith in themselves and in the Creative Power, enabled them to develop the talents, skills and abilities to make it come true.

What we are saying here is that whatever you desire right

now can become a reality. If you desire wealth, you will be led to the circumstances which will make you a fortune. If you desire friends, you will be led to the right people. If you desire a new job, you will be guided to the right employment. But this must be done through your Creative Imagination.

Secret #8
THE GOLDEN KEY
OF CREATIVE
IMAGINATION

All the world's a stage,
And all the men and women merely players...

Shakespeare

In the theater, a 'dream' is created which, if conforming to the Aristotelian concept of dream, the audience accepts as 'reality.' The limitations we have set upon ourselves are just as unreal as what is happening on-stage, for we have chosen to embrace that which is fictitious. But while we must accept the reality of the *moment*, we are not bound in it *forever*. We can change the future through the use of our imaginations.

The personal limitations you have accepted can be broken any time you wish. By persistently imagining what you really want, you can discard the old script and introduce a completely new story. In other words, you can free yourself of the handicaps that are holding you back.

IMAGINATION CONTROLS THE WORLD

"More important than knowledge is imagination." This statement was made by one of the world's greatest scientists and mathematical geniuses, Albert Einstein.

The power of imagination is one of the greatest forces in the universe. Human progress has developed in direct proportion to the collective imagination. In my travels, I never cease to be amazed at the enormous network of airlines. What great imagination it has taken to put them together! Each phase, from man's first flight to the multi-dimensional concept of mass air travel, had to be an idea in someone's imagination before it could become reality. Like all visionaries, those who dared to conceive had to break through the limited thinking of those who declared their ideas impossible.

Leonardo daVinci wrote these prophetic words on his sketch of the first flying machine: "Man shall grow wings." His machine did fly a few feet but Church leaders of the day, labeling it an instrument of the devil, forced him to destroy it. Time proved daVinci right. Now men and women truly do have wings!

The most dynamic aspect of imagination is the act of forming mental images of what does not yet exist in the physical world. Another power is creating new ideas and combinations of ideas stimulated by and based upon previous experience. *Creative imagination* takes us a step further than just forming mental images. It causes things to come into existence, it makes or originates, it produces and brings about. When we are creatively imagining something, we are actually causing it to come into being because it has been formed, for the first time, in our minds. Our images contain *creative power*. They are changed through the power of creative intelligence.

The actual means by which things come into being in the outer world is a mystery. Yet we know that if we plant a kernel of corn in the earth, it will produce a stalk with several ears of corn on it. We do not know nature's secret for drawing the substance from the soil to make this new creation. The *image* or *picture* of the stalk of corn is *locked* within the kernel.

An idea is like the seed you plant when you want a certain crop. It will produce *whatever you plant*: corn, wheat, tomatoes, weeds, thistles or poisonous nightshade. Everything depends upon the *nature of the seed*. Whatever idea you hold in your imagination, whether it be negative or positive, constructive or destructive, it *will bring forth its own kind*. Like attracts like or, to quote the philosophers, "As above, so below."

Creative imagination is a powerful force. The industry of the entire South was changed by one man's creative imagination. One evening as he sat in his home, he watched his cat trying to pull his canary through the bars of its cage. As the bars protected the canary, the cat only succeeded in getting a paw full of feathers. This caused the man to visualize an iron claw pulling cotton from a cotton plant. And so it was that Eli Whitney invented an amazing machine: the cotton gin.

The creative imagination can be used to overcome world problems. We must never think of any situation as hopeless or unresolvable. The belief that we are on the path to self-destruction is simply not true. There have been prophets of doom and gloom since the beginning of recorded history, but they have been wrong every time. When things looked the bleakest, along came individuals with creative imaginations who led us to even greater achievements.

All problems are really *opportunities* in disguise. The Chinese realized this: Their symbol for crisis is made up of two other symbols: one for problem and one for opportunity. Bearing this in mind, it behooves us to carefully examine every so-called crisis in our lives for the hidden opportunity in it.

THE CONSCIOUS PHASE OF MIND POWER

The conscious phase of mind power is the most limiting because it is dependent on the outside world. Its information comes through the five senses: hearing, tasting, smelling, feeling and seeing. Since our senses often deceive us, we frequently accept false concepts, values and beliefs.

The conscious mind is objective. It observes, is rational, is where our will-power comes from and may be likened to a guard at the door. Protecting the access route to the subconscious mind, the conscious mind screens all incoming data and allows the subconscious to accept only that which it perceives as the truth, no matter how faulty.

What we see with our conscious mind often deceives us.

We look at the horizon and the sky and earth seem to meet; a rainbow seems to disappear into the ground; railroad tracks seem to come together in the distance. These distortions are the result of false images and messages from our conscious minds. Relating this concept to the human predicament, sickness, poverty, worry, despair and hopelessness are faulty images we have accepted from our conscious minds and chosen to perpetuate in our subconscious minds.

To free ourselves from the limitations of our conscious minds, we must turn *within* for here is the source of truth. It is not in the outside world. To continue to look for it externally is to continue to experience those conditions which have been holding us back. For this reason, we must listen to the Superconscious Mind within, take that information into our conscious minds and, to create positive and constructive experiences, deliberately program it in our subconscious minds. To do this, we need to take a better look at the Genie within.

WAKING UP YOUR GENIE

In the story of "Aladdin's Lamp," we are told of a genie who carried out any wish Aladdin had. All Aladdin had to do was rub his lamp and the genie would appear. *You* have a far more powerful genie within you right now, ready to carry out your every command. But, because you are unaware of this, he has been sleeping for many years. The time has come to wake him up!

Throughout the centuries, successful people have either *intuitively* or *knowingly* become aware that they too, possessed a power that would serve them just as the genie served Aladdin. They called on this power to help them create great works of art, compose, invent, write, build businesses, etc. Biblical scribes knew about this power when they wrote, *"as you think in your heart, so are you."* Using 'heart' as a synonym for 'subconscious,' what they were really saying was, 'as you think in your subconscious mind, so are you.'

Although superbly talented and possessing unlimited ability, your subconscious is a *servant* and, as a servant, must be COMMANDED. It can't motivate itself. In fact, it is an *automatic impersonal mechanism* which will *faithfully* bring about whatever you most persistently impress upon it. It is a valued, competent, trustworthy partner which will supply you with all the necessary information you need to function in a positive, creative manner.

Remember, we said that your subconscious responds according to the beliefs and convictions you hold in your conscious phase of mind. Your conscious mind chooses what it believes to be true and your subconscious accepts, without question, whatever it dictates. Your subconscious will, therefore, accept failure as readily as success and is, indeed, the *means* which will bring about either one.

At this very moment, your subconscious is working for or against you. Through your conscious mind, it senses and records all your physical, intellectual, mental and emotional experiences and stores the information for further use. The sum total of these experiences determines your present level of Awareness.

Warren Hilton wrote in *Applied Psychology*:

Considering from the standpoint of its activities, the subconscious is that department of the mind which, on one hand, conserves, subject to the call of interest and attention, all ideas and complexes not at the moment active in the consciousness. Observe then, the possibility that lies before you. On one hand, if you can control your mind in its subconscious activities, you can regulate the operations of your bodily functions, and thus assure yourself of bodily efficiency and free yourself from functional disease. On the other hand, if you can determine just what ideas shall be brought forth from the subconscious into the consciousness, you can select the materials out of which will be woven your conscious judgments and emotional attitudes.

THE CORRECT THINKING PROCESS

As we have said, our conscious minds are greatly influenced by our five senses so it is easy to see why we get confused when we use the conscious mind alone to bring about the right answers to our problems. The five senses do not report the truth to us most of the time, so we accept, reject and relate everything based on what may be a *mistaken certainty*. To look at a situation and evaluate the information based on the conscious mind alone is to look at the *effect* instead of the *cause*. This makes us value-judge both ourselves and others and evaluate what we see, hear and feel as if it were, indeed, the truth. The lives of so many people are plagued with one problem after another because they take actions and make decisions based on their faulty Awareness.

What we need to do is to train ourselves to look *within* and ask our Superconscious Minds for guidance. As long as we rely on the conscious mind alone, we shall continue to make mistakes and become disappointed and frustrated.

The correct thinking process goes like this:

1. Go to the Superconscious Mind to get the correct guidance.
2. Use the conscious mind to program this information into the subconscious.
3. Command the subconscious to carry out this information.

FACTS YOU SHOULD KNOW ABOUT YOUR SUBCONSCIOUS

1. Your subconscious is only stable and effective in direct proportion to the quality and clarity of the information supplied to it by your conscious mind.
2. Anything you picture vividly in your mind will be brought forth by your subconscious and become a reality for you.
3. Your subconscious will draw to you what it clearly understands to be your desire.
4. Your subconscious doesn't reason why, but records with high fidelity anything and everything your conscious mind presents to it.
5. Your subconscious will draw to you the circumstances, people and conditions to fulfill your desire.

6. It will not fulfill your goals or desires automatically. You must ask it and tell it exactly what you want.
7. When you ask it, it will alert your conscious mind to recognize the right opportunities, people and circumstances needed to fulfill your desire.

HOW TO PROGRAM YOUR GENIE

Your subconscious responds to three things:

I. VERBALIZING:

There is a tremendous power in words. Words can build or destroy your life. They made you what you are right now. The Bible says, "Every word that shall come from thy mouth shall not return unto you void."

Talk is verbalized thinking and you utter about 20,000 words a day. The way you talk to yourself has a profound effect upon your feelings, actions and accomplishments. What you say determines practically everything you do. For instance, words can even change blood pressure, heart beat and breathing.

The subconscious accepts without question the words we use to program it, whether they be positive or negative. Positive statements or affirmations build your life while negative statements or affirmations destroy it. Take a moment right now to think about this. Do you use any of these negative affirmations:

> *I don't like my job.*
> *I worry a lot.*
> *I'll never have any money.*
> *I can't quit smoking.*
> *I just can't get along with that person.*
> *I don't have as much get-up-and-go as I used to.*
> *I don't have enough time to do what I want.*
> *I don't have any patience.*
> *That's the way I am.*
> *I don't have any special talents.*
> *I need a rest.*
> *I'm not perfect.*
> *I can't lose weight no matter what I do.*
> *I've got too much to do.*
> *I have trouble meeting new people.*
> *I have a poor memory.*
> *I always get a cold in the spring.*
> *I don't feel very good.*
> *I can't remember people's names.*

Of course, the list could go on and on but it is long enough to show you how we program ourselves. The subconscious is then *required* to carry out these negative commands and so we experience sickness, lack, limitation and failure.

What you must do is to police your speech and turn such self-defeating statements around. The way to program your mind is to use positive affirmations and repeat them over and over again until your subconscious accepts them as reality. In psychology, this is called the Law of Predominant Mental Impression. When you keep saying that you are sick, your subconscious is *required* to make you sick; if you affirm health, it is *required* to make you healthy. Never rehearse a contrary situation by saying to yourself that you feel great, then, the next minute when someone asks how you are, telling them you feel terrible just to get their sympathy. Switching back and forth only confuses the subconscious, and this will have repercussions in your life.

II. FEELING AND EMOTION

Emotion is the carrier of creativity. No creative act is performed without it. The subconscious responds greatly to feeling and emotion. Repetition, by itself, has little effect, but a word of caution: negative emotions and feelings, such as fear, anxiety, frustration, jealousy or hate, will work with just as much force as their positive counterparts. This is why they are so destructive.

Speaking aloud or listening to music while using repetition to impress an idea in your subconscious will increase the intensity of the vibrations and help you impress the information more quickly. Psychological studies have shown that this can be done eighty-five percent faster through the use of music or voice recordings.

III. VISUALIZATION

Everything starts in the mind. It is imperative that you understand this. Imagination or visualization is the picturing power of your mind. Your subconscious responds to pictures and images held on your mental screen. It may be said that your subconscious is the contractor which will build your life. You are the architect and your imagination, the blueprint.

You are constantly running a mental movie with yourself as star of the show. These images determine your personal behavior and the kind of life you lead. You have the power to mentally create a new life for yourself. Whatever you visualize, you can have. All you must do is see yourself as having achieved your desire. Once you do this, CONSIDER YOUR WISH ACCOMPLISHED. For you are a self-fulfilling prophesy. What you are thinking about today is a clear indication of where you will be experiencing in the future.

Visualize yourself having, doing or being the things you want. Feel yourself enjoying them. See the details—colors, places and people—as vividly as you can. Hold the pictures clearly in your mind. Most important—you must put yourself in the picture. Get yourself a scrapbook and call it "Blueprint of Destiny." In it, put colored pictures of the things you want, the places you want to go or the things you want to do. Look at the pictures every day and let them seep into your subconscious. Soon, you will master the technique of visualization and, in the process, desire will become reality.

THE SUBCONSCIOUS— A CREATIVE AUTOMATIC MECHANISM

You can train your subconscious to perform any act you consciously choose. When a great pianist plays with ease, you can be sure that he has spent years building habit patterns of perfection in his subconscious. His subconscious mind stores these memories and releases them under automatic control so that he does not have to consciously think which key to depress each time he wants to play a different note.

Your subconscious is an automatic mechanism which will solve your problems and change your life much faster than your conscious mind alone. Further, it is never limited because it can be trained and retrained. Just as long as you keep on picturing what you want, like a submarine torpedo programmed to seek out an objective, it will forget mistakes, change course, correct itself and bring you right on target, all automatically.

YOU ALREADY HAVE IT

The key to releasing your subconscious power is to get the feeling that it's working. You must, therefore, picture the END RESULT. Feel that you can get what you want. Feel that it is ALREADY YOURS. Feel the enjoyment . . . the excitement NOW.

Your limiting conscious mind may conspire against you through your intellect. It may tell you that what you desire cannot be achieved; that it is impossible. Do not accept this as the truth. Instead, *remember that you will get what you want when you feel as though you already have it*.

If you want a new automobile, go to a dealer and get some brochures. Examine the pictures. Stop in at the showroom frequently and look at your car. Visualize and imagine yourself in it. START BEHAVING AS IF YOU ALREADY OWNED IT. *Act* as though you had just been told it had been shipped and would be delivered soon. Even buy something to go with it.

Give thanks in advance. Now this may seem strange if you do not understand the principle. But by giving thanks in advance, you are positively acknowledging that what you want is on its way to you. Once you accept this, conditions will commence to change because you will be reaching for a higher dimension of consciousness than that in which you have been operating. You will be in a state of magnetic attraction.

Secret #9
CHOOSING YOUR DESTINATION

Successful living requires that you devote yourself to fulfilling a worthy life plan. If you do not consciously commit yourself to the personal response-ability of giving your life purpose and direction, you will be like a ship without a captain to steer it or a chart to follow; the kind of vessel destined to end up shipwrecked on some desert island. For a ship without destination flounders at sea and is lost.

In life, so many opportunities needlessly pass us by because we do not know where we are going. There is an intelligent Force in the universe which is unfolding a Master Plan for creation. You are part of that plan. If you look at the stars, animal and plant life and the sea, you will observe that they are all components of a very orderly universe.

Everything has a place and a reason for being. Projecting the macrocosm to the microcosm, you, too, have a place where you *and you alone* fit in an orderly and desirable way.

It may well be that your problems exist primarily because you are not in your right place. There are things you should be doing which you are neglecting or avoiding. You don't fully appreciate the fact that you are a unique individual with a special place to occupy and a purpose to fulfill. Your contribution to life may not seem great but, as part of the Supreme Architect's plan, you are, none the less, just as important as the most prestigious person you know of.

Everything worthwhile that has happened throughout the ages is part of the Creative Plan. All the world's great achievements, in every field of endeavor, have been made possible because individuals have listened to Inner Guidance which manifested a strong desire and inspired them to set out to achieve it. To others, these desires may have seemed futile. But those who create have both *purpose* and *direction*. They realize that they are not merely corks floating aimlessly on an ocean, but individuals in full control of their destinies.

Several studies have shown that individuals who have a definite plan for their lives are happier and more successful than those who do not. It is tragically true, for example, that the major difference between people confined to mental institutions and those who are not is that, almost without exception, the inmates have no plans or goals.

At this stage of your development, it is important for *you* to make a plan for *your* life, one which will utilize all your talents and abilities. You must *take the time* right now to figure out what you want to do and how far you want to go. Otherwise, like the captainless ship, you will end up useless to yourself and everyone else.

Each area of your life should be planned so that you can judge if you are making progress. How can you possibly know if you are succeeding if you don't establish a goal? Set up your talents and aim straight for them. Once you begin doing this, you will discover the pleasure, satisfaction and value of making detailed plans for the things you want to accomplish.

One of the basic secrets in achieving our objectives is to break our big goals into a number of smaller ones. Nothing is really difficult if it is broken down into parts. As each part—each short-range goal—becomes a reality, the satisfaction derived from its attainment is a spur to the next milepost. Failing to understand this principle, many people resist establishing large goals because the total effort involved in achieving them seems overwhelming. A single glass of water can form a dense fog. If you break down the water into sixty-thousand million drops, it can cover an entire seven-block area and extend to a height of one hundred feet. The same is true of your efforts. If applied each day, in the end, they will make equally as great an impression.

In the game of goal-setting, one hundred percent success is *not* a requirement. Even if you don't achieve everything you set out to do, you will still be further ahead than if you just did nothing, as is the case with so many people. It is a fact that goals, whether they are realized or not, constructively change people's lives. They direct our mental energies into positive channels. All it takes is to know what you want to have, what you want to achieve and what you want to be.

WHAT WILL YOU HAVE?

You can have anything out of life if you will be *definite* about it. Most of the time, we are far too vague in identifying precisely what we want. Thus, many of our goals die in the realm of wishful thinking. People often say to me, "I don't know what I really want." This is just another excuse to escape the personal responsibility of handling their life. To never make a decision is never to make a mistake! Their fear of rejection or failure and need for approval hold them prisoners.

Not to decide is to decide, for choice is inevitable. Not to choose success is equivalent to choosing failure. And indecision creates frustration. We know we should be doing something creative but, instead, settle for indecision and feelings of self-doubt and inadequacy.

You will feel a tremendous surge of self-confidence and power if you just take the time to choose a worthy goal, and make a plan for your life. After selecting your goal, evaluate it before presenting the plan to your subconscious. Use the screening process below and ask yourself—

1. Do I really want this?
2. Is it right according to my value system?
3. Is it realistic?
4. Can I visualize it in all respects?
5. Will I be a better person when I accomplish it?
6. Do I have complete faith that, with God's help, I will succeed?

If you answer 'yes' to all of these questions, than your next step is to make plans. To do this you must—

1. Have a clear statement of your goal. Your subconscious responds to definiteness. Be definite and businesslike.
2. Have an exact time and date to begin your program.
3. Have a *written* plan of action.
4. Have a schedule to periodically review your plans for changes and updating.
5. Carry a brief statement of your goal on a 3×5 index card and look at it often each day. If possible have a picture of your goal on the card.
6. Concentrate on one specific need or challenge at a time.
7. Make up a positive affirmation or statement about your goal.
8. Always go to sleep picturing your goal.

GET THE WRITING HABIT

Most people do not bother to write down an exact description of what they want. At one time, in my lecture work, I distributed worksheets to help people do this, yet less than five percent ever actually used them. Most intellectually agreed that the idea was a good one but felt the details involved were too much bother. After all, they knew and could remember what they wanted to do. This attitude is one of the major reasons why only five percent of the people on this planet are successful. They are the ones who are working with and not trying to beat the success system.

People say, "I can remember it." But can they? Can you? Let me give you an example. How much do you remember of what you read on the first two pages of the previous chapter? Don't worry about it! You can always go back and look. After all, it is WRITTEN DOWN in black and white.

When you write your plan down, *print* in BOLD LETTERS. Do not type. Each day look at it.

But why do all this? It is a psychologically sound principle that *vision* accounts for approximately eighty-seven percent of your total sensory perception. Further, kinetic energy from the act of writing down your plan impresses your sub-conscious deeper than if you just thought about it. Remember when you misbehaved in school and the teacher made you write something a hundred times? The teacher knew that you would tend to remember what you *wrote down*. The subconscious mind catches up with written instructions, incorporating the information in the automatic structure of the brain and central nervous system, already making it a reality.

You will find the following worksheet helpful in mapping out your CREATIVE PLAN OF ACTION.

DIRECT ACTION WORKSHEET

THIS IS MY GOAL (Write a brief description) _____

_____

ATTACH SKETCH, PICTURE OR *CLEARLY* WORDED DESCRIPTION
BELOW

WHY DO I WANT THIS? _____

HOW WILL I BENEFIT? _____

WILL IT HELP OTHERS? _____

WILL IT BE RIGHT LEGALLY AND MORALLY? _____

ADVANTAGES _____

HOW CAN I REACH MY GOAL? _____

_____

WHERE CAN I GET COMPETENT INFORMATION AND GUIDANCE?

_____

DATE OF *INTENDED* COMPLETION _____

I WILL REVIEW & REVISE ON THE FOLLOWING DATES _____

_____   _____   _____   _____

WHAT SHOULD I DO FIRST? CHECK WHEN STARTED & FINISHED

1. _____START _____FINISHED _____

2. _____START _____FINISHED _____

3. _____START _____FINISHED _____

I MUST KEEP THE FOLLOWING POSITIVE MENTAL ATTITUDE DURING THIS PERIOD.

(Make a positive statement concerning how you feel you must *act* while you are working on your goal.)

SET GOALS IN THE
SIX MAJOR AREAS
OF YOUR LIFE

You need to make plans for each of the six major areas of interest in your life. These can be classified as follows:

CAREER: What do you want to accomplish
                  as far as your work is concerned?

FINANCIAL: *Realistically*, how much money
                  do you want to have?

PHYSICALLY: What program for physical fit-
                  ness do you want to develop?

MENTALLY: In what areas of your life do you
                  wish to study and obtain more
                  knowledge?

FAMILY: What relationships do you want
                  to have and maintain with your
                  family?

SPIRITUALLY: What are you striving for spirit-
                  ually?

These goals can be broken down into long-term and short-term goals. Make a list of your *ultimate*, *long-range* goals, and, also the *short-term* goals you are going to act on *right now*.

GIVE YOURSELF A FIVE-YEAR PLAN FOR GROWTH

In addition to completing the Direct Action Worksheet, take a blank piece of paper and write down a five-year plan for growth. Call this your *Blueprint of Destiny*.

On your Blueprint, set down a plan which will involve new mental and spiritual viewpoints, new environment, new work, new friends, higher income and a better standard of living. Make this an outline of the best life you can possibly imagine for yourself.

Begin to look for related opportunities which will help you reach your goals and check your plan frequently to see that you are on the right path.

Keep revising this Blueprint for the rest of your life. Consider it an unfinished symphony; one on which you are constantly working but determined to complete. You will be richly rewarded.

START WHERE YOU ARE

One of the greatest discoveries you will ever make is to learn to live in the present; to live a day at a time. *NOW* is the only time there is, yet we insist on wasting it by mentally living in a past we cannot change or in a future which we long for or dread. In establishing your goals, you must be careful not to get caught in this trap. All consideration of yesterday must be expunged from your memory. And the future, which is not yet a reality, must not be ransomed. It must be free to use when it becomes the present.

Many people live in the future and neglect what should be done today. While *planning* for the future is vitally necessary, living in it only produces frustration, anxiety and failure because, by doing so, one is escaping from immediate reality.

To live a balanced and creative life, you must get into the habit of doing those things which are before you today, and doing them as efficiently as possible. If you learn to perform your present task well, no matter how unpleasant it may be, you will have taught yourself a valuable lesson in personal growth. Although people often delude themselves into thinking that they can do a better job at something else, there is a Universal Principal which states that you will not be given greater opportunities in life *until you have proven that you are more capable than your present work demands*. Read this again! Failure to perform your present actions efficiently and successfully will delay success and may actually set in motion a situation which will cause you to go backwards. Do not try to escape from the present for a better future that does not yet exist. *Your present task is the most important thing you have to do.*

NOT HOW MUCH BUT HOW WELL

The Creator has a Master Plan for the universe which far exceeds our understanding. As channels for creation, He constantly seeks to unfold his Perfect Plan through us. For this, He needs our cooperation. By learning to grasp the productive opportunities that are before you each day and utilizing them to the best of your ability, you are contributing to the creative process. Unless you cooperate, you will never be able to express your unlimited potential because you will be working against, not with, the creative process. Hence, it is not a matter of how *much* you do but how *well* you perform each action. In other words, it is the *quality* of your performance that matters.

GETTING YOUR PERSPECTIVE

The attainment of goals *per se*, impotant as it is, must not be permitted to overshadow or obscure their real objective: to give your life *purpose* and *direction*. That is why you must be careful not to let them *lock you into the future* and keep you from living in the *now*.

After you have chosen your goals and set up a program of action, you must learn to relax and allow your new Awareness to carry you forward, patiently doing what is necessary, first things first, *with no fear or concern about what is going to happen in the future*. As the spiritually-oriented say, "Let go and let God." By so doing, you will be aligning yourself with reality and keeping yourself open to the intuitive Guidance from within which will show you each step of the way.

Inner Guidance is always available. Seek it out and use it. If you don't, your Awareness may not yet have the wisdom to chart a course which is in full alignment with the Creative Plan for your life and you will continue to be disenchanted and disappointed when things do not work out.

When you make plans and set goals, you must first meditate and ask the superconscious what you should do. Present ideas you have consciously thought out and direct your superconscious mind to guide you in selecting the right one. You will soon get a feeling about what you should do. Trust your intuition. It will never let you down. Then *act at once*, always remembering that you must leave yourself open for changes along the way. The first move, however, must be yours. You will not be guided unless you demonstrate you want guidance.

Keep in mind the Biblical admonition, "With all they getting, get wisdom and understanding." It is best not to ask for *things*. Don't ask for a new car, money or a new home. Ask for the *wisdom* necessary to go about getting these things. If your ambition is to be an artist, actress, business executive, or anything else, ask for the *wisdom* to guide you in achieving it. Wisdom is the *only* thing God has to give you. You must use it and do the rest yourself. You can pray your heart out but God, who must rule His Universe by Law, cannot change things just for you. Only by gaining wisdom, will you know how to work with the Law and bring forth your desires.

Go forward a step at a time and remain flexible to change. You may not reach your original goal but, instead, may be guided to *something better*. In either case, you will experience a feeling of excitement and personal fulfillment. Instead of pushing yourself into a situation which will only cause you frustration and misery, your intuition will guide you to your rightful place where you can be supremely happy.

Compare life to a train ride. If you want to go somewhere, all you have to do is to get on the train and stay there until you arrive. The train may stop or change tracks but, *if you stay with it*, you will eventually reach your destination. If you keep getting on and off you may never get there.

To reach your destination, you need do only four things:

1. Decide to get on the train. CHOOSE YOUR GOAL.
2. Choose the best possible route to get where you are going. THE RIGHT PLAN.
3. Pay for your ticket. BE WILLING TO PAY THE PRICE FOR WHAT YOU WANT.
4. Get on the train. GET INTO ACTION.

Your train is waiting right now. It's time to get aboard!

YOU ARE WHERE
YOU WANT TO BE

Like it or not, at this moment you are *exactly where you want to be*. Perhaps you are unhappy. You may have a job you hate, a marriage that is deteriorating, a love relationship that seems to be going down hill, or a family relationship that is unsatisfactory. Your future may look doubtful but you, and you alone, have *chosen*, consciously or unconsciously, to allow yourself to be right where you are. The evidence indicates that YOU WOULD RATHER BE IN THAT SITUATION THAN PAY THE PRICE TO CHANGE.

Your spontaneous rebuttal may include such excuses as, "You don't understand." "My situation is different." "I'm trapped where I am." "I want to straighten my life out, but I can't because . . ." And you may be quite sincere in these contentions. But the fact remains: *you have permitted your present environment to limit your thinking.* By choosing to let a person, circumstance or condition dictate your happiness, you have abdicated your life to something *outside* yourself. In effect, you have declared that your situation is greater than the Power within you to change it. Your subconscious has brought the negative affirmation you have developed and, as a result, is obediently delivering exactly what you asked for.

RESPOND TO LIFE WITH ACTION

"What holds attention determines action"
William James

A weak, timid, indecisive approach to life breeds inertia, failure and disappointment. Many people fail to act because they are afraid to make a mistake or think that what they conceive can never become reality. Great inventions and discoveries go unrecognized when those behind them give up in despair, exclaiming, "My idea hasn't a chance!" This attitude is tragic because the world needs what each one of us has to offer.

Back in 1880, a man employed by the US Patent Office handed in a letter of resignation. "Everything has been invented that could possibly be conceived of by man," he wrote, "and I see no future in my job." Don't be like this man! The future is full of unlimited opportunities for those who take *action* and turn their thoughts into realities.

FORTUNE FAVORS THE BOLD

Remember this psychological truth: FORTUNE FAVORS THE BOLD. You must conceive in your mind the world you want to live in, the situations you want to master, and the greatness you want to achieve. The ideas and concepts for releasing your unlimited potential can only be turned into reality if you take bold action *now*. Wishful thinking will not make your dreams come true. Learn this lesson from history: "He who hesitates is lost." Undoubtedly, you could relate dozens of instances in your own life when you hesitated and lost. But you won't ever have to be a loser again if you learn to take *bold action*.

If you want to be free, your thinking must control your limitations instead of your limitations controlling your thinking. Look at your life for a moment! What do you see? Do you see opportunity, love, happiness, success and fulfillment? Or have you mentally set up restrictive limitations? If so, the fact that you have declared yourself a prisoner will make you a prisoner. Once you make up your mind to be free and tell yourself that you are "sick and tired of being sick and tired," you will be motivated to make necessary moves towards liberation and find a way to cease being "sick and tired." The truth is: you will *remain* where you are only as long as you wish.

The interesting thing about this is that you do not have to be superhuman or extraordinary to break loose from your limitations. There is really no such thing as a "great" person. There are only "ordinary" people who have *decided* to do "great" things. These are people who are motivated by a burning desire to be free in order to express their unlimited potential. Each day, they meet their problems head-on, overcoming them *one at a time* until they achieve their deepest desires. Instead of blaming others for their condition, they start out *doing something* constructive about their situation.

Apply this to yourself. Your personal freedom and innermost desires are waiting for you, but first, you must STAKE YOUR CLAIM!

MAKING FRIENDS WITH FAILURE

Failure is a necessary part of growth yet it produces one of the strongest fears most people have. As a child, it didn't bother you. If you were skating and fell down and bruised yourself, you got up and started to skate again. Did you consider yourself a failure every time you fell down? Of course not!

Everything you learned as a child was learned by trial and error. Sometimes you were successful, and sometimes you weren't. If you weren't, you simply tried again until you got it right. You didn't condemn yourself or withdraw and resolve never to try it again. Failure was accepted as part of the growth process.

Unfortunately, somewhere along your path of development, you picked up the idea that there is something wrong with failing. You became very much concerned about what others would think when failure occurred. Your need for approval was starting to develop. Even if you did nothing with your life, you felt you must always look good in the eyes of your family, friends and society.

You may have decided that the best way to avoid failure was to tackle only those things for which success was assured in advance. Since there is very little in life that we can be one hundred percent sure of, your activities would necessarily be limited. This attitude probably had its genesis in your teens when you were striving for the acceptance of your own peer group. You would rather have died than appear inadequate or ridiculous.

It was then that you spent a lot of time comparing yourself to others. Someone else always had assets you felt you didn't have. Therefore, in order not to expose yourself to challenge, and the possibility of failure, you began to withdraw. Failure was something which must be avoided at all costs; approval was your strongest motivation.

As this habit pattern became impressed into your subconscious, limited thinking made you a prisoner. In order to function, you created a *comfort zone* whereby you avoided the unpleasant and established a routine you could tolerate. Unfortunately, your comfort zone shut off all the unlimited possibilities which existed outside it.

If you are to break out of the comfort zone you created, you must make friends with failure. When you decide to give up your need for approval, it won't matter how many mistakes you make as long as you reach your ultimate goal. Thomas Edison conducted 10,000 experiments before inventing the lightbulb. Undeterred, he didn't classify any of these experiments as failures for he had successfully identified 9,999 ways his invention wouldn't work!

A solid base for your goal is *persistence*. This is the dynamic quality which separates the achievers from the nonachievers and often, surprisingly, takes the place of intelligence, knowledge, education and even experience. Those who are persistent refuse to allow any circumstance to get in their way. An unknown writer put it this way—

Nothing in the world can take the place of persistence. Talent will not. Nothing is more common than unsuccessful people with talent. Genius will not. Unrewarded genius is almost a proverb. Education will not. The world is full of educated derelicts. Persistence and determination alone are supreme.

THE LAW OF EXPECTANCY

Time and time again, psychological studies have shown that the basic reason for a person's success is that he *expected* to succeed. Athletes who achieve success expect to win. Take Mohamad Ali. In his usual, out-going way, he customarily affirmed victory by stating, *"When* I win the fight..." not "If I win this fight." Now, that's total self-confidence!

Aristotle said, "What you expect, that you shall find."

Expectations control your life, so it is imperative that you control your expectations. If you expect the best, the best you shall have. But if you expect the worst to happen, be assured that it will. By permitting your life to be dominated by negative thought patterns, you form the habit of expecting negative results. Studies show that ninety percent of people have negative expectations.

You may find this hard to accept but the reason you grow old is because you expect to. You have been programmed to begin getting old when you reach a certain age. At that point in time, you take on, without question, the personality, dress style and symptoms of old age. Elephants have an instinct which enables them to predict death. When they feel their time has come, they embark on a journey to the elephants' graveyard. The majority of people I know do about the same thing!

Total self-confidence is built through *positive expectations*. You can build positive expectations by knowing that you have the power within to overcome any obstacle that lies ahead. So many people have a magnetic attraction to the past. They save momentos, clippings, old letters and trivia, and keep scrap books. If you want to succeed, your mind must be geared to the future and these things replaced by pictures of what you want to accomplish; by visions of *expectation* of the great events which lie ahead.

When you find it necessary to reminisce, try to recapture some of the more pleasureable expectations you had as a child or young adult which have become reality. Build on these and bring them up-to-date. See where your expectations have brought you and make plans to go on to better and better achievements.

Look forward to the future with expectation, then act

enthusiastic. Enthusiasm is a powerful motivating force; the little-recognized secret of success. Derived from two Greek words, 'en' meaning 'in' and 'theos' meaning 'God,' *enthusiasm means God in You*. And it is this God Power within you which will enable you to accomplish anything you desire if you release it through dynamic thinking.

The margin of difference in actual skill, ability and intelligence between those who achieve and those who fail is really quite small. If two people are evenly matched, the one who is enthusiastic will find the scales tipping in his favor. Even an enthusiastic person with second-rate ability will often succeed where a person of first-rate ability, lacking enthusiasm, will fail.

When Mark Twain was asked the secret of his success, he replied, "I was born excited." Thomas Edison said, "When a man dies, if he can pass enthusiasm along to his children, he has left them an estate of incalculable value." And Emerson, in his essays, observed, "Every great and commanding moment in the annals of the world is the triumph of somebody's enthusiasm." The respective life experiences of these men bear out their shared philosophy.

When you expect something positive, through the Law of Expectancy, just like a magnet, you will attract whatever you expect. If you open your mind to better conditions, know that they are on their way right now. For your expectations of today will be your life of tomorrow.

THE SECRECY PRINCIPLE

None of your time should be spent in telling others what you are going to accomplish. To do so is tantamount to seeking their approval. By disclosing your goals, you will, on the one hand, dissipate valuable energy needed to accomplish them and, on the other, set up opposition from those who wish to control you. They will try to talk you out of doing what you feel you must, frequently to justify their own inertia.

Most people have low self-esteem and poor self-images. They dislike seeing anyone having more or do better than they and will resort to almost any extreme to put down someone who tries to break away from mediocrity. Don't give them a chance! Many would-be achievers have lost out before they even got started by letting others, particularly family members, talk them out of what they really wanted to do.

The Master Teacher said over and over again, "Tell no man!" The Master Teacher taught his followers to turn within; to shut the door on outside opinions and appearances and talk to the Father. He was referring to the secret place within your own consciousness; the very core of your personality. Unless you are sharing a goal with someone else, it is best to keep it to yourself.

Secret 10
YOU DESERVE A
BREAK TODAY

The best break you can give yourself is one devoted to meditation with its unique combination of peace and power. Persons concerned with the betterment of humankind have come to the conclusion, at different times and in different places, that, if we are to achieve our maximum mental, physical and spiritual potential, a system of complete rest, relaxation and inner communication is essential. Without this, we can only expect to operate at a fraction of our capabilities.

Different techniques have been developed to help us reach our potential. The most common is *meditation*. Its forms range from yoga with its various branches to commercial mind-control courses, biofeedback and transcendental meditation. All have much in common.

It must be stressed from the beginning that meditation is not the invention of any one group or individual. It does not necessarily have anything to do with any religious group or denomination. No initiation is required, no ceremony is necessary and, contrary to what you may have been led to believe, no one has to teach you how to meditate. While instruction may be helpful, it is not essential.

All the mystery and hocus pocus surrounding meditation has kept many people from exploring the possibility of integrating it into their lives. The simple fact is that the art of meditation can be learned with little or no difficulty by anyone. For the ability to meditate is inherent in each one of us. Once we understand the basic principles, we can meditate by ourselves.

Many would-be practitioners run into trouble right from the start because they permit themselves to be indoctrinated into believing that a particular method of meditation is the *only* one to follow. This simply is not true. Research studies, conducted at several universities, have failed to prove that *any* system is superior to another. Each one strives to achieve a state of relaxation and inner communication and, if each is followed sincerely and conscientiously, the results will be exactly the same. Beware of any system which says, ours is the *best*. There is no "best." All will work if you give them a chance.

The contention that meditation must be taught on an individual basis is unsupported. I regret to say that all such individual training does is to serve to justify the exorbitant fees charged for instruction. I stress this point because so many people have spent large sums of money only to realize afterwards that the expenditure was unnecessary. I have personally taught thousands of students to meditate at group sessions and have achieved exactly the same results as when I taught individually.

Actually taking one of those commercial meditation courses is like using one of the new fully-automatic cameras. The cameras are set for *average* conditions. But there is really no such thing as an *average* condition, just as there is no such thing as an *average* person. You will never see a creative photographer using such a camera. He makes his own settings and adjusts for the conditions of the moment.

Nothing is right for everyone, every time. The more you use meditation, the more personal the technique becomes. And, like the creative photographer, you are thrilled with the mastery of your own choice of "settings" and the results you finally achieve.

WHAT IS THE PURPOSE OF MEDITATION?

Meditation reestablishes our contact with the Source of Power within us. It cleanses the mind and makes us open and receptive to creative ideas, intuition and inspiration. It reveals where we have gone wrong and guides us back to the right path again. We become one with everything and everyone because, as we meditate, we tune into One Mind of the universe. It helps us to achieve our full potential through deep rest of the nervous system, rest which is deeper than ordinary sleep but, throughout which, we *remain alert*. During this time, stress is released and we are fully relaxed and calm. Just as an athlete runs to train his body, in meditation, we are tuning and training the mind to function at its maximum potential. This is one of the basic reasons why meditation increases efficiency in everyday life.

HOW DOES MEDITATION FEEL?

Meditation is a kind of mental, physical and spiritual recharging where you feel totally at peace and calm within. At some time or another, each one of us has experienced this feeling without actually knowing what it was. After meditation, body motivation and senses are intensified: you like more, do more and feel more. As you continue the practice, you are able to handle problems and troublesome situations with new calm, poise and self-assurance and take complete charge of your life.

WHAT ARE SOME OF THE SIDE EFFECTS OF MEDITATION?

Meditation has *no negative* but many *positive side effects*. These are natural and are present in all forms of the art when the student is meditating properly. Here, then, are some of the beneficial results you may experience as a student of Positive Meditation.

1. Most medical authorities today will agree that a dominant factor in all successful healing is the patient's *desire* to get well and his *belief* that he can get well. The process becomes one in which the patient heals himself with the help of a skilled physician. Positive Meditation is thus encouraged. Numerous instances have been recorded where the healing powers of the body were accelerated to such an extent that tumors, which had previously resisted treatment, disappeared in a short time. And, surprisingly as it may seem, cases of terminal cancer were reported cured when Positive Meditation was used as a last resort.

2. Oxygen consumption decreases about twenty percent. This decrease is as much in ten or fifteen minutes of meditation as it is in eight full hours of sleep.

3. Lactic acid salt particles in the blood decrease by fifty percent. This is vitally important for it is lactic acids in the bloodstream which cause a person to become fearful, worried and anxious. Lactic acid salt also causes unnatural fatigue and paves the way for serious physical disorders.

4. The body has a much greater resistance to germ invasions, colds, viruses and other disorders of the head, throat and lungs.

5. Drug addiction, including heroin addiction, has been reported cured within a three-week period when the addict's resolve to "kick the habit" was reinforced with Positive Meditation.

6. Cardiac output markedly decreases. This indicates a reduction in the workload of the heart.

7. When compared with sleep or drowsiness, meditation gives deep rest *clearly* and *distinctly*. Deep rest is experienced simultaneously with expanded awareness.

8. Intelligence and learning ability increase because meditation synchronizes electrical waves in the left and right hemispheres of the brain.

9. Produces superior psychological rest and causes the heart to maintain a restful pace even *outside* meditation.

10. Gradually brings about a permanent and beneficial reduction in the heart rate so that there is less wear and tear, and improves cardiovascular efficiency both during and after meditation.

11. Stabilizes the nervous system so that there is more resistance to environmental stress, psychosomatic diseases and behavior instability.

12. Meditators recover from stress more quickly and reveal more favorable responses to stressful stimuli.

13. Speeds up reaction time which indicates increased alertness.

14. Performance in certain situations is faster and more accurate because there is greater coordination between mind and body.

15. High School students have exhibited growth in their intelligence rate. They performed better in recall tests, learned more quickly and grades improved sharply.

16. People show greater increase in job satisfaction and performance, along with improved relationships with co-workers.

17. Self-image improves markedly within a short period.
18. Level of depression is significantly reduced.
19. Majority of asthmatic patients show improvement.
20. Significant reduction in the use of alcohol, cigarettes and non-prescription drugs.
21. Significant reduction in allergies.
22. Students display a growing interest in the tendency toward normalization of weight.
23. Meditators are able to solve problems better and reveal a more organized memory.
24. Meditators show improved athletic performance and ability.

Let us stress again that these are *side effects*. Some organizations use them as selling points to induce the public to take their courses. Although they do provide motivation for many people, they are not the primary *purpose* of meditation. The real purpose is to bring you closer to your internal Source of Power. If you keep this as your major goal, the side effects will be automatic. If, instead, achieving one or more of these becomes your purpose, you will miss the whole point of the experience and be greatly cheated in the process.

WHEN TO MEDITATE

Begin by putting aside a time for meditation at the beginning of each day, preferably before breakfast. This will tune you into the Life Force and program you for the day. Then set aside a similar period in the evening. It is suggested that this be at least four hours before retiring because you will automatically be rejuvenated. Concentration on goal-setting may keep you awake if you meditate too close to bedtime. Some, however, enjoy a period devoted to peace and tranquility just before dropping off to sleep. Your night-time meditation will help you get rid of the negative feelings you have accumulated during the day.

This or a similar schedule should regularly be followed for best results. Meditating once a day is better than meditating twice a day every other day, or every third day. What you are looking for is the cumulative effect. Continuity is an important factor in achieving best results.

One never actually stops meditating. It is an unending process. It is as necessary to life as breathing, and those who are not practicing it intelligently and effectively are choking for life. Once you start meditating properly, you will never be the same again. The whole idea is to make it a permanent part of your life.

It is a demonstrated fact that most schools of meditation have a high percentage of failures among their students. Most people who take such a course, generally at a cost of hundreds of dollars, become, for a time, fervent meditators. However, after a few weeks or months, they practice med-itation less and less and soon give it up altogether. For this reason, if you decide to make meditation a part of your life, I recommend that you make up your mind from the begin-ning to do it every day regardless of what else you have going. Never say you haven't time. You must *make* time. If you meditate sporadically, the results will be minimal.

HOW LONG SHOULD ONE MEDITATE?

Meditation should last for about fifteen or twenty minutes. Although there is no set time, this has been found to be the most effective period of time. During meditation, you will begin to feel better than you ever felt before and, as a result, will be tempted to meditate longer than necessary. But, as with everything else in life, you must use common sense. There is no virtue in over-long meditation. The object is to make contact with your Source and receive illumination and inner guidance, not to see how 'high' you can get.

WHERE SHOULD ONE MEDITATE?

I assume that you will be doing most of your meditating at home. Find a place where you can be alone, preferably in a room where you can shut off most of the bright light. A quiet spot is essential, one where you can keep out the noise of the world. Noise saps your memory and kills your chance of being able to concentrate and communicate with your higher mind.

It is a good idea to meditate in the same location each day. After a while, you will build up a kind of positive vibration there which will help promote relaxation. You will automatically associate that spot with being quiet and peaceful.

The spine should be straight so that the nervous system is not pinched but able to function at its maximum freedom. A comfortable straight-backed chair is good for this purpose. It will keep you from hunching over and help distribute your body weight evenly. Try different chairs until you find the one in which you are the most comfortable and unaware of your body.

Do not lie down. To do so will only make you associate meditation with sleep. Eventually you will just doze off and miss out on all the benefits for which meditation is intended.

BEFORE YOU START

The most important thing to remember at the outset if this: DO NOT FIGHT YOUR THOUGHTS. Many people say, "I have trouble meditating because I can't stop thinking." Their problem is resistance. The more you resist your thoughts, the more they will get in the way. But once you stop resisting them and let them pass by without giving them your DOMINANT ATTENTION, they will cease to intrude.

The first thing to do, then, is to slow down your mind, body and senses. You are trying to form a kind of vacuum which can be filled with creative thoughts and vibrations. If you start thinking that the house needs cleaning or the shopping done, stop immediately and discipline your mind to return to meditation.

Meditation is like changing the direction of a wheel. First, we have to slow down the wheel. After we slow it down, we stop it and then start it rolling the other way.

Your subconscious mind will help you in this process. Once it knows what you are trying to achieve, it will create a habit pattern which will enable you to reach this state of consciousness. Just keep on programming the new habit into your subconscious and this will be done automatically without any distracting effort on your part.

In order to achieve this peaceful feeling, you may wish to read something illuminating before going into meditation. If so, read for a few minutes until you *feel* calm. Then close the book and try to *hold the feeling* but *not the thought*.

This experience is rather like starting a motorboat. If you have ever done this, you know that the first time you pull the cord, the motor doesn't start. You try again and, all of a sudden, it catches and you're off. And so it is with meditation. After you have experienced this feeling a few times, it probably will not be necessary to read before going into meditation. This is not to say that you shouldn't read if you still want to. Whatever helps you to relax is beneficial.

Meditation is a three-step process. The first step is to *relax and let go*. The second is to *reach out and listen*. And the third to *visualize and affirm*. The following method consolidates, in simplified form, all the latest findings and techniques established by psychology, religion, Far Eastern philosophy and medicine.

STEP ONE

RELAX AND LET-GO

As long as your muscles are tense, they absorb both physical and mental energy. To get rid of this distracting electrical energy, stretch out your entire body and make all your muscles loose. Then sit upright in your chair and close your eyes.

Take a deep breath and exhale, slowly and comfortably. Feel yourself relax. It is normal to relax when exhaling. Now flex or tighten your muscles by squeezing them and letting them go. Start with your arms, hands and shoulders. Next, do the muscles in your back and abdominal area. Finally, those in your thighs, calves and feet. Take another deep breath and relax.

At this point, some organizations give their students a 'mantra,' which is a meaningless phrase whose purpose is to keep the mind from wandering. The mantra is supposed to be specifically designed to correlate with the student's present state of consciousness. But each time we meditate, we are at different states of consciousness so a pre-selected mantra is really of no value. Anybody who tells you that you *must* use a certain mantra, based on a few minutes of conversation, is pulling your leg. The only reason a mantra will work is because you believe it will.

The best phrase I have found is LET-GO. Just say to yourself LET-GO. Take another breath and repeat the words until you feel yourself letting go of all your concerns, anxieties and negative thoughts. Keep on repeating them until you are calm and peaceful and your mind empty of all conscious thinking. At that point, you will be open and receptive.

STEP TWO

REACH OUT AND LISTEN

This is a mind-expanding function. Every great thinker, philosopher, theologian, mystic or scientist has disagreed with his colleagues on many things but the one thing on which they all agree is that there is only one Mind in the universe. This one Mind—the Superconscious Mind—is the origin of all thought.

Your direct guidance and intuition comes from the Superconscious Mind through the subconscious mind. Remember that the subconscious is open at both ends. At one end, there is the inflow of creative ideas from the Superconscious and, at the other, the instructions from your conscious phase of mind. Your reasoning or conscious mind tricks you by distorting your perception of reality causing your Awareness to be faulty and, subsequently, your actions. In order to connect up to the one Mind, the one Force, the one Life which expresses itself as you and through you, you have to move your conscious mind out of the way. It's as if you owned and controlled a great Power House in which a tremendous electric dynamo waited to serve you at your turn of the switch. Once you allow this one Mind to dominate your consciousness, life will be a fantastic experience.

It is not necessary to try to understand the Superconscious or figure out how it works. All you have to know is that it exists and will guide you, allowing you to float through any of life's problems or obstacles. Spend a few minutes meditating on the fact that the same force which sustains the sun, clouds, planets and sea is *within you*. Know that you are an expression of that Power. Know that it is perfect. Let your mind float in it. Give it a chance to enter and illuminate your consciousness. *Know that you are one with that perfect, unlimited Power*.

If you have any need in your life or problem to which you are seeking a solution, briefly state it. Note, I said *briefly*. You are dealing with an all-knowing Intelligence so you really don't need to tell *It* anything. The "telling" is for *your* benefit. After you have done this, RELEASE the thought. Let your mind act like a radarscope and sense its directional influence. Be open and receptive to whatever intuition or guidance you receive.

Learn to take a listening attitude as if you were expecting to hear something. As I said earlier, sometimes it is difficult to meditate when you are thinking about your need or problem. But, in effective meditation, you set the details aside until you have prepared yourself, then you release them and listen. Meditation is a time to silence your distracting thoughts and empty your mind of its routine, mundane distractions.

With practice, you will suddenly become aware that you are listening. Guidance will come through *intuition*. When you receive an impelling urge, you will feel a sudden impulse to act: to do something, to contact someone or go somewhere. This is your cue. This is your direction. TRUST

IT. ACT ON THIS GUIDANCE. It can *never be wrong* for your subconscious is connected to the Source of all-knowing Intelligence.

Do not reject some things because you do not like them or because they are not what you think they should be. Beware of your conscious or reasoning mind working against you. Carry out your guidance *absolutely*. When you get suggestions to go somewhere or do something, go where you are told and do what you are impressed to do. Let your subconscious take full charge. If you do, you will meet people you need and they will help you. I have experienced this hundreds of times.

For example, try this. When entering a room, ask your subconscious who you should sit next to. You will be prompted to approach a certain person and will find that this person is the one with whom you should be. He or she is either someone who can help you or someone to whom you can offer help.

Sometimes, during meditation, you may be prompted to pay a debt instead of buying something you want. Don't worry about it. After you have paid the debt, you can still have what you want because your subconscious will help you to acquire it. Just *listen to*, *accept and do* exactly what your intuition tells you. If you are told to leave something alone, leave it alone. If you are told to change something, change it at once. You cannot alter your life by doing only the things you like and neglecting the rest.

A young lady who attended my lecture class in Chicago wanted very much to visit Hawaii. She had neither the money nor what seemed like the means to get it. She meditated on this and was prompted to visit a travel agency for brochures. She did so and even started buying things for her trip. A short time later, she received a call from a friend who wanted to vacation in Hawaii but didn't have anyone to travel with and would pay her fare if she would go along. Because of her actions and willingness to follow the guidance of her subconscious, this girl was prepared to accept the fact that she would make the trip. Most people would have forgotten about the whole thing, but she trusted her subconscious.

STEP THREE

VISUALIZE AND AFFIRM

Take a few moments and visualize and affirm whatever it is that *you* want to be, do or have in *your* life experience. Any words repeated over and over again with conviction and authority in this state of consciousness, especially if they are linked with visualization, will infallibly be experienced.

Picture a mental screen before you. You can change your life by seeing yourself acting out those things you want; by altering your images of mind. The secret is to visualize yourself as *already having these things*. If you want health, picture yourself as perfectly healthy. If you want money, see yourself with lots of money, spending and enjoying it. Picture your bankbook with a large balance. If you want your business to expand, note the increase in customers. In each situation, see yourself as smiling and happy.

Visualize your wishes as clearly as possible. Not only

see them but *feel* them. They are already a reality once they have been visualized for that is the law of Mind. Do you remember Professor James' words? "The greatest discovery of our age is that man, by changing the inner aspects of his thinking, can change the outer aspects of his life."

Reinforce the images with positive affirmations or statements which relate to what you wish to accomplish. You can select from those listed in the last chapter of this book, or make up your own. Keep on repeating them silently while visualizing. Remember always: words have *creative power*.

Finally, mentally *give thanks that it is so*. This will make you consciously aware that your desires are on their way and will create a feeling of expectancy. This is absoslutely essential to their realization. Open your eyes and stretch, enjoying the feeling of a project or desire now assured of completion or attainment.

The more you meditate, the more you will like it. The less you meditate, the more you find it a bother. The more you do it, the greater will be your rewards. Every successful person since the beginning of time has discovered this simple truth.

Secret #11
THE TIME OF
YOUR LIFE

In the lives of busy people and in those of many of us not nearly so busy, no question is asked more often than, "Where has the time gone?" Time, of course, does not depart the scene as the question suggests but merely moves on at its normal rate while we become painfully aware that we are accomplishing much less than we should. "Time is money and must be spent wisely," another authority observes. We've been told this all our lives, but have we any choice not to spend it? Of course not! Unlike the time-keeper at a sports event, in the game of life, we can't 'stop the clock' for instant replay. And when we protest, "I don't have the time," more often than not the truth is that the project at hand has not a sufficiently important place in our priorities to warrant our *taking* time for it.

155

Let's admit it. No one has more time than another. We have the same amount of time in every day as everyone else; the same number of minutes in our hours. And, yet, we repeat the same old phrases.

In striving for a fuller, more complete and satisfying life, we hear alot about regarding stewardship of wealth and possessions. Less is said about the stewardship of talent. And little about the stewardship of time. Yet these and all life's 'gifts' carry with them certain built-in responsibilities.

Unquestionably time passes quickly. Every moment that goes by is a time in our lives. As our entire existence is composed of time, it is of the utmost importance that we consider the emotional significance of its usage. "I'm awfully busy," "I'm in a hurry," and "I just haven't the time," are three large nails in the coffin of happiness. Continually rushing through life precludes the development of a personality of strength and beauty, and robs life of its savor and flavor.

Every morning beyond our bedroom windows lie fresh air, trees, mountains, fields or parks. But we rarely ever see them. We turn right over and go on sleeping or simply jump out of bed and rush off to work. There just seems to be no time to enjoy nature's beauty. And when asked why this helter-skelter, progressless pace, modern life provides reasons galore. We need only turn on our television sets and be assailed by the multitude of commercials wherein a myriad of physical and mental afflictions are dramatically and sympathetically presented in an effort to sell the great cure-all, and to find justification for failure and procrastination. However, when we take time to face up to reality, remorse over time wasted can be acute.

What is needed then is release from the tyranny of the

clock. You must learn to master time instead of being mastered by it. Stop being time's fool. Neither waste it nor get caught up in the 'no time' syndrome. Instead, learn to control it and make time for the important things in life. When you snatch the whip of hurry from the hand of time, you will regain self-mastery.

IS TIME THE PROBLEM...
OR YOU?

There are very few time-conscious people. Everyone wastes time and most of it is just frittered away until the box score and time-remaining-to-play indicate we're involved in a losing game. We are gripped by a feeling of inferiority. This is followed by a sense of inadequacy and fatigue. The relentless ticking of the clock holds the impression of failure before us and the ability to manage our lives is impaired.

Take you, for instance. There are things you've been meaning to do for years: learn a language, make a dress, visit some place, write a special letter, take a course, finish a book, do . . . . If only you'd more time! You're soooo busy. But are you . . . really?

TIME MANAGEMENT
VS.
SELF-MANAGEMENT

People take courses in time management and still end up having no time to do the things that are necessary for success. If you really want to get something done, you'll find the time to do it. You don't need a time management expert to tell you how. Let me give you some examples.

Presume I'm going to hire you to sell cosmetics. In the next forty-eight hours, I'll give you one hundred dollars for every lipstick you sell. How much time are you going to spend on eating, talking on the phone, watching TV, engaging in idle conversation or just sitting around during that time? Would you talk with anyone who isn't a good prospect for your lipstick?

Okay, you're in school. For every "A" you get, I will give you a check for five thousand dollars. If you maintain a four-point average, I will give you one hundred thousand dollars. Do you think you could find the time to study?

If these offers were made to you, you wouldn't have to read a book or take a management course to find the time to do a good sales job or attain high grades, would you? The reason for this is simple. You would have identified an extremely desirable goal and have an almost uncontrollable obsession to achieve it.

There you have it! The secret of finding time to do the things you *want* is *wanting*, not *wishing*, to do them. We all *wish* we could do more but actually don't *want* to, so we just keep on wasting time and wishing for more of it. This is ridiculous!

When we do make a decision to master time, the first step is not, as many suppose, that of tackling the nearest calendar and budgeting our days. This is the last step. The first step is to clarify why we want to do something rather than why we ought to do it. This is done by developing a real philosophical understanding of the importance, as well as unimportance, of time in our lives. Given the emotional motivation to take command, the mechanics of achievement will follow.

Gaining the upper hand of the clock and calendar in no way implies disregarding time. Only when we know how to deal with it are we in a position to evaluate it correctly. By working with time, we can achieve remarkable results. But easy does it! The first attempt need not involve mountain-moving. The secret of winning is beginning. And, once we have time on our side, our simplest efforts will accumulate the strength and vigor needed for any greater effort.

EVERY JOURNEY BEGINS
WITH A
FIRST STEP

Do you want more time but don't know where to begin? Make an effort to rise earlier! This one step can add one or two hours to your productive day and years to your life. Take on something you have been meaning to do and do it in your spare time before breakfast. Would you like to be an expert on some subject? Every morning study for a half hour and you can become an authority on it. That's all it takes. It's so simple, it escapes the majority of people who keep chanting, "Someday I would like to..." "One day, I must...but I never seem to have the time."

Just because you never started the work, play or study that really interests you is no reason why you can't start right now. Time doesn't count us out. We only imagine it does. It's never too late to begin. Time is impersonal. It is the same every moment. It imposes no limitations upon us. Our only limitations are self-imposed.

Admittedly, it is difficult in this frenzied modern world to avoid being caught up in a sense of urgency and hurry, but we can often normalize the accumulating pressure by throwing our minds and nerves into neutral and coasting for brief periods of quiet meditation midway through mornings and afternoons.

THE "AFTER THEORY"

You can achieve success in anything if you are determined to make the time. Instead of bowling every week, wny not bowl every other week? Instead of going to the same place every week, why not go every other week? By saving an evening, you will have time to do other, more important things.

Most people live by the 'after-theory.' They've got real plans. They're going to do great things...*after* the kids grow up, *after* they change jobs, *after* they get a new car, *after* they finish school, *after* they get new drapes, etc., etc. This 'after' period never comes but they keep on promising themselves that, some day, they are going to get what they want. Now while opportunity may knock more than once, it seldom sits on the doorstep awaiting our pleasure. And, sooner or later, we experience frustration and discouragement.

Do the things you always wanted *now*. Or make plans *now*. Or program your subconscious *now*. Not tomorrow! You will never have more time than you have today. How you spend the next twenty-four hours is what counts.

Get the feeling of adventure. On your next day off, take a trip to the park, mountains or a nearby seaside resort. Never mind the weather! Get up and get out!

Use your imagination. Think about getting a ticket to some place, packing your suitcase, slamming the door and escaping from the dullness of everyday routine. Even if the journey is short, think of the thrill of saying, "I'm going away next week."

Want to travel to foreign countries? The stepping stone is making time. Plan and get going. Don't wait a moment longer. Once you get the feeling that you are going to make something happen, it will. Traveling will become a part of you, and you will have a strong desire to see more and more of the world.

Feeling is the key to expectancy. Get the feel of the moment; the feeling that this is it. That you are going to break out. Expectancy will set in motion a mighty power within you that will cause your desire to happen. The more excited you become, the faster you will get your wish. By maintaining this state of consciousness, you will draw to you the ways and means for bigger and better adventures.

DON'T LET TIME MANAGE YOU—MANAGE IT!

Frustration and discouragement are always homemade. With a little thought, we find that time, without its whip, is a great encourager. Our job is to learn to love time; to value it for the value it brings.

Time has meaning only when it holds experiences that impress; when it expands life's meaning for us. It seems to drag or fly according to what it holds. Once we grasp this, we begin to master the role it plays in our lives, creating time as and when we want it.

Let me give you an example of making time. My first love is lecture work. I do over two hundred lectures a year and love every moment of them. I have never been trained as a writer, so I find writing very demanding on my abilities. Yet I have trained myself to write through discipline.

Because I would rather be lecturing, I must make time to write. And this book was important enough to me to make that time. For two months, I shut myself off from the rest of the world to complete this goal. The rest of the world and my friends thought I was dead. I only worked on the manuscript. After all, what are two months out of my life when the results may benefit many people?

Although I was dead to everyone else, I was very much alive in what I was doing. My excitement and enthusiasm were self-created and enabled me to complete the book. In essence, writing the book demanded discipline, making time and creating the excitement and enthusiasm which carried me through.

So many people are bored. They say there is nothing to do. How sad this is! They drink, play bridge, knit and do almost anything for the sake of killing time. But while they are killing time, they are also killing their creative imaginations. They have no time for study, meditation or self-improvement. As has been observed so wisely, we are taught to save time and waste our lives.

Life is to act. Not to act is death. The clock is ticking away. Life is an emergency. The time is now.

Visualize yourself as a person who always does things now. Everything you envision is done right away or, at very least, you make plans to do it right away. If you really want to be emotionally strong, healthy, successful and alive, find time to study and meditate on the principles we have been talking about. It takes time to be successful. Lots of time. There is no magic formula. It takes time, study, meditation and action.

Make use of the time God has given you. Most people do not realize the value of time until they come to the end of it, then they beg for a few minutes more. Those who died in the last twenty-four hours would have given anything for another twenty-four hours. You can spend the next twenty-four hours reaching your true potential or sliding down into your own particular hell. The choice is always yours.

Suddenly you will begin to realize that a correct sense of timing is nothing more than an instinctive response to the moment, governed by innate good taste and common sense. You will experience a new sense of control. You will learn to relax tensions that prevent the smooth interaction of mind and body. The more you experience a sense of correct timing, the more self-confident you will become. One of the basic characteristics of a successful person is their instinctive sense of timing. As a deliberate act, timing is studied by actresses, radio and TV performers, artists, dancers, writers, comedians and . . . lecturers.

I am very time-conscious because I have to be. I check my watch just before I go on stage. My mind is on the present moment. I quietly think about the audience which will be mentally linked with me in the next few minutes. I think about how they will be able to benefit from what I am about to share, and how I will benefit from their receptivity. And I time myself accordingly.

When I finish speaking, people come up and thank me. I receive thousands of letters. It's all worth it. It isn't a waste of time because I'm having the time of my life!

TIME BECOMES A TOOL, NOT A TYRANT

You must learn to regard the clock as an artist regards his materials; not as a whip but as a paintbrush to add beauty to the picture you are creating. You must be aware of the freedom of choice you are exercising and learn the value of time without fearing it. In other words, you must do whatever you do because you are using time for your purpose or objective, and, in no case, permit it to be an end in itself. There is no virtue in budgeting time unless you get more out of it that way.

Using time effectively depends largely upon learning to set priorities. One of the simplest but finest methods of doing this is to get into the habit of writing down each night before retiring the six most important things you want to do the next day. After you list these, put them in their order of priority. As you get those things done you set out to do, you will be filled with a great sense of accomplishment. Each project you complete will make the next seem easier. And success will follow success.

Allotting one's hours to their best use is a splendid mental exercise because, in so doing, one must decide on the relative importance of items to be included in any day's program. This type of preliminary evaluation, which helps separate essentials from non-essentials, guarantees rewards way out of proportion to the initial time involved. The ancient Chinese proverb says, "A journey of a thousand miles begins with a single step." You must not only start moving, but keep moving *forward*.

Manage the time you have allotted efficiently. There is no need to rush. Some people are always in a hurry but never seem to get any more done than those who pace themselves. Do you remember when you last wanted to 'save time'? What did you do with the time you saved? Did you put it away to use some day when you needed it? The point is that time can be managed but not saved. Trying to save time only results in anxiety and frustration, which you don't need. Remember our earlier precaution. Don't save time and waste your life!

Making use of time begins with realizing how you are presently using it. Look over your daily activities and see where you can make changes.

Do the most unpleasant jobs first. This way, you will

work harder and get more done because you will always have a pleasant task ahead.

Take time to make time. Don't forget to make time in your schedule for planning.

THERE NEVER WAS
A BETTER TIME—
FOR YOU

Because we exist in a universe of magnificent rhythm and timing, the body and mind respond easily to the rhythm of repetition in action. In your assumed mastery of time, never regard regularity as a mundane, dull, uninteresting matter of duty, but think of it as the same type of rhythm that makes music enjoyable. The challenge and invitation are to swing along with it and catch the tempo of the melody of life. One of the principal objectives of this book is to help you build more self-confidence so you can enjoy the
TIME OF YOUR LIFE!

Secret #12
OVERCOMING FEAR AND WORRY

Fear has been around for thousands of years that we know of. Our primitive ancestors feared thunder and lightning; feared the wild beast and feared each other. Fear was present when Noah launched his Ark. The word appears in the Bible over four hundred times. When nations are at war, the world fears an expanded conflict. When there isn't a war, we fear the war that might be. In between, we fear a thousand and one things, large and small, involving ourselves, other people and situations in our daily lives.

We were born with only two fears: the fear of falling and the fear of loud noises. The rest we developed ourselves, through our own efforts. Fear takes many forms. There is claustrophobia which is the fear of confined spaces; agoraphobia, the fear of open spaces; ailurophobia, the fear of cats; astraphobia, the fear of thunder and lightning; hematophobia, the fear of blood; acrophobia, the fear of heights; hydrophobia, the fear of water; nucophobia, the fear of darkness; and the worst phobia of all, the *fear of failure*.

Fear is a destructive emotion which deals a fatal blow to any attempt on your part to build total self-confidence. If you are afraid, it is impossible to have the positive mental attitude essential for successful living.

REVERSE, NOT REHEARSE, YOUR FAILURES

By giving your *dominant thoughts* to failure, you are impelled to fail. Failure is rehearsed by constant repetition. How many times a day do you think about failing and failure? Do you ever tell people that you know you are going to fail? Do you find yourself thinking, "What a terrible failure I've been," "I can never do anything right," "I don't have enough education," or "I'm not very attractive?" This is the kind of negative rehearsal which, when combined with early childhood training, makes you respond to the greatest challenges and opportunities with, "I can't!"

How do we remove fear? A positive mental attitude will motivate you to overcome fear. Removal starts with a positive belief about yourself. Know that, within you, is a Power greater than what lies before you. Use positive affirmations to reinforce your belief until your subconscious accepts it as fact, and fear is replaced and eliminated.

The next step is to be willing to *face* failure. Before starting on a new endeavor, ask yourself, "What is the worst that can happen?" Be prepared mentally *should* failure occur. It is important here to distinguish this from expectation. I am *not* saying that you should expect to fail, for this would make failure certain. What I *am* saying is that if you are mentally *prepared* for the worst, you will have the confidence to enable you to meet and successfully handle even the greatest of challenges.

We worry about many things but they all boil down to this: WE ARE NOT LIVING IN THE PRESENT TIME ZONE. Now think about it. You can only worry if you are either mentally living in the future which you long for or dread, or in the past where what has happened is disturbing you. If you are living in the present, it is *impossible* to worry. For instance, are you worried this very moment? Of course not! Why? Simply because you are reading this book and your concentration precludes worrying. The mind cannot think of two things at the same time.

Overcoming fear and worry can be accomplished by living a day at a time or, better yet, a moment at a time. Just say to yourself, "For the next few minutes, hours or days, I will . . . !" Make a positive statement and keep your promise only for the time limit you set yourself. Forget about the future beyond that. If you live life a piece at a time, your worries will be cut down to nothing.

It is important to have a sense of humor. Humor is a safety valve. It keeps you from taking yourself too seriously. The problem with most people is that they take life too seriously. Even religion is too serious. What should be light, exciting and uplifting is a guilt-producing experience. If you make people feel unworthy, you can control them. It's the old situation of dependency. But surely God must have a sense of humor. If you look at the aardvark or porcupine, it is not hard to conclude that He has. He gave us a sense of humor to relieve our tensions. Humor is centered in tragedy. It allows us to laugh at our fears.

Do whatever you fear the most. Again and again, plunge into the very thing which makes you afraid so that, in the end, your fear will be eliminated. Using fear as a means of conquest helps to build spiritual and emotional muscle.

Most of the time fear is due to using the mind more than the body. If you *think* too much and *neglect* action, you generate fear. Lead a more active life and you will have less time to worry. Take long walks to release body tensions. An over-active mind and an under-active body can lead to trouble. On your walk, *take this book with you*. Find a quiet spot, take a break and, without looking, open it. Your sub-conscious will guide you to the right spot. Read a page or two and then take the long way home. As you stride along, thinking about what you have read, your mind and body will be working in perfect *balance*. Fear starts when there is a lack of balance. This principle has been recognized in developing the body but completely overlooked in developing the mind and bringing the two into harmony.

CHANGE, THE ORDER OF THE UNIVERSE

Mental hospitals are filled with patients who are unable to face change. These people have created ways to try and escape from it. But if there is one thing even more certain than death and taxes, it is the inevitability of change. No one can avoid it. So we must learn to accept and look forward to it.

In fact, change is what you *want*. You want to be somebody instead of nobody. You want to be important; to matter. You want beauty in life; champagne instead of beer; an automobile instead of a car; a home instead of a house. And you can only have all these things if you relinquish fear.

Change means changing your way of thinking. It's also being willing to give up things the way they are to have them the way they can be! No one else can do that for you. While this book may provide the guidelines, it is you who must act.

CHANGE COMES WITH BEING DIFFERENT

Make no mistake about it, if you are to escape from behind the negative barriers you have constructed, you must consciously decide that you *want* to be different. *All great individuals are different*. They are different from the masses. This is what makes them stand out.

You must have enough guts to say to yourself, *"I will not lead a life of mediocrity. I am different. I am a fantastic person with a fantastic future. A dull life is not for me."* Repeat these statements. Don't wait! Start right now! If you are alone, stand up and shout them out! The clock is ticking and time is wasting. From now on, you are going to think, speak and act positively and not let the fear of failure and the future control you.

If you are exhausted and fearful, perhaps there's no adventure in your life. Nothing is worse than being in a rut. To sleep in the same bed every night, eat at the same restaurants, see the same people, go the same way to work, do the same thing every day is *complete madness*. Sameness destroys creativity and will quickly have you banging on the psychiatrist's door. People caught up in this cycle are the 'Some-day-I'm-going-to-ers' I spoke about earlier. They are the slaves to sameness; the ones who fear the slightest change.

When you are frustrated with your daily routine, change it. Changing does not mean putting everyone else aside or feeling superior to family and friends. It means claiming the right to speak and act for yourself and doing what is necessary to make *you* happy. Confucius summed it up this way. "They must often change who would be in constant happiness." When you are happy, those around you will benefit.

The first thing to do is to stop fighting change. Learn to live with it and enjoy it. The weather is going to change. Your company is going to change. The government is going to change. So are the people around you and your community. Everything and everybody is going to change, so why fight it? Why not be one of those who says, "Let's see what I can change to improve things?"

Make the *right* changes. The right changes are always positive. Begin by changing small things every day until change becomes a way of life. Don't cling to one lifestyle. Change the furniture . . . your style of dress. Change something. Switch things around in your room, apartment or house. Don't leave anything the same.

Do you find yourself resisting this? If so, like the 'Some-day-I'm-going-to-ers,' you feel threatened by change. Remember, the only way to overcome fear is to do the thing you fear the most. And if that's change, then change you must!

Change your hairdo and color. Try some new foods. If you are dissatisfied with your looks, consult a plastic surgeon. Read Dr. Maltz's book on Psycho-Cybernetics and see how he altered thousands of lives. Let him tell you in his own words what a new appearance will do for your personality. Surprise yourself and your friends with the changed you.

Change is a habit. Your whole life is lived by habit. Since infancy, you have trained yourself to respond the way you do. Changing your life means unchanging your habits. Sometimes this can be unpleasant, but it will only be temporary.

To overcome apprehension, keep in mind the ultimate *benefits* you will receive. Concentrate on the benefits instead of on the fears and assumed hardships which change might impose. Write these benefits down. Read them each day and see what change is doing for you.

Look at everything that comes into your life as a chance to change *for the better*. If you are about to be transferred, or if your office or department is closing down, your job position has been eliminated, your husband or boyfriend wants to move, your lover has left you, you have to move to a new place or your car has finally stopped running, instead of dwelling on the negative aspects, think of possible positive consequences. If you stop resisting, accept the change and look forward to a new and better experience, something good will happen. Good comes when you are ready to change.

Secret #13
MOVE AHEAD THROUGH POSITIVE COMMUNICATIONS

One of the most common phrases I hear in my counseling work is, "We just don't communicate." Because most people identify communication with the written and oral word, they often feel that they are not communicating. But this is not the case at all. They are always communicating. People communicate through body language, facial expressions, gestures, mannerisms and even silence. Their ability to communicate shows just as much in what they *don't* say as in what they *do*.

In America, we do little to develop non-verbal communication. In some cultures, such as the Oriental, considerable emphasis is placed on non-verbal communication. The Japanese have a word for this: harrigay. Derived from two other words, 'harra' meaning stomach and 'gay' meaning art, harrigay is the art of getting inside another person and trying to understand her or him with little use of the spoken word. A person is responsible not only for what he says, but for what the other person *understands* through gestures, mannerisms, expressions, body language, etc.

If you are having problems communicating with others, the first thing you must understand and accept is that *you* are the problem. It's all tied in with the way you come across, and the way you non-verbally communicate to other people. All family problems, business communication gaps, individual misunderstandings and even wars are rooted in our inability to understand another's point of view. So let's begin by recognizing the fact that we cannot change others but we *can* change our attitudes *towards* them.

Communication is a delivery system for our attitudes. The way we express ourselves is an outward manifestation of what we are thinking inside. Longfellow wrote, "A single conversation across the table with a wise person is better than a ten-year study of books."

One of the greatest problems which threatens any marriage occurs when both partners have not learned *how* to communicate with each other. Most failures in business are not really business failures at all, but *people* failures. People just fail to communicate. Almost every study shows that employees view a good manager as one who can communicate with them. A poor manager may spend more time with his employee but less time in communicating. Able to communicate, the successful manager can elicit his subordinates' ideas, so time spent is more productive.

Each one of us is a manager. You may be managing a business, family, job, education or a friendship. To be successful, each of these requires positive communication. Here are some ways in which you can be more effective.

LISTEN—LISTEN—LISTEN

Nothing is more important in communications than listening. There is the old story about two women walking down the street and they ran into another woman. One of the women engaged herself in conversation with the third for a full ten minutes. The first woman observed while the second did all the talking and the third all the listening. When they finally parted, the second woman exclaimed to the first, "That's one of the most brilliant women I know!" "But," protested the first, "she hardly said a word." "I know," said the second, "but she listened. That shows she's smart!"

Developing a listening skill will prove that you, too, are smart. We all feel that anyone who has the good sense to listen to what we have to say must be a good friend. Listening has become a lost art. Notice when you are talking to some of your acquaintances. They can't wait for a pause so that they can say what is on their minds. They really don't hear you. They are too busy rehearsing what they are going to say next.

It has been established in the study of Extrasensory Perception (ESP) that if you send an ESP thought and there is no one to receive it, it simply does not exist. In other words, there has to be both a *receiver* and *sender*. The same goes for conversation. If someone is talking to you and you are not listening, the conversation does not exist.

Listening is by far the most vital characteristic of good communication, but it is also the most ignored. A large portion of our lives was spent in learning to read, write and talk but no time in learning the art of listening. Most of us just want to talk, and if people don't listen, we get very upset. "Why aren't you listening?" or "You're not paying the slightest attention," we say.

Whether you are aware of this or not, the way you listen has a greater impact on others than the way you talk. The world is crying out for good listeners. Nothing threatens another person's self-esteem more than indifference. But good listening extends beyond mere silence. Signs of irritation and boredom, sarcasm, thoughtless interruptions, disagreeing with what a person is saying and not placing any significance on what is being said all play their parts in self-erosion.

When you act this way, the other person feels rejected. Inside, he is saying, "I have something to say that's important. I need to be heard." And that person will be heard, if not by you, then *by someone else*! He will do whatever is necessary to make someone listen. The child may throw a tantrum, spill something or fight with his brothers or sisters. The student may skip class or refuse to study. The marriage partner may use the silent treatment or stay away from home. The employee may gripe or complain. Each one will find a way to be heard.

For the most part, people do not communicate as such. They simply take turns talking! Many wouldn't listen at all if they didn't have to. And herein lies the problem. Few people truly want to listen or improve their listening ability.

This was proven to me a short time ago when I offered to teach two courses at a local nightschool. The courses—the first on public speaking and the second on listening—were so set up to prove a point. Within a few days, the 'speaking' courses were completely booked up. As a matter of fact, I had to conduct two classes to accommodate the crowd. As for the 'listening' course, not one person enrolled! Everyone wanted to talk, but no one wanted to listen.

If you think about it, who are the people you hold in highest esteem? They are those who will listen to you. We are attracted to people who want to hear what we have to say. This is why so many psychiatrists and psychologists do such a booming business. People want someone to listen to them even if they have to pay fifty dollars an hour for the privilege.

In order to be a good listener, you must *want* to be a good listener. Each person with whom you come into contact must be made to feel important. If the head of an organization or some social or political figure whom you hold in high regard wanted to talk to you, you would be all ears. But if a street sweeper, housekeeper or dishwasher wanted a few minutes of your time, would you be as attentive? Probably not! Yet if all these people were to disappear for a week, who would you miss more? The important authority figures or the people who make you life more comfortable? The point is that *all* people are important and you should let them know this by listening to them.

By *wanting* to be a good listener, you will find out how fascinating people are. People you may have taken for granted or considered dull and insignificant suddenly become interesting. Indeed, there are no uninteresting people; only disinterested listeners!

WE ARE MORE INTERESTED IN OURSELVES THAN ANYONE ELSE

This is a simple fact of human nature. We have feelings, emotions, pride and anxieties. But so does everyone else. In order to develop positive communications, we have to TAKE AN INTEREST IN OTHER PEOPLE. It is not necessary to be clever, make smart remarks, tell great stories or prove how intelligent we are. What is necessary is that our approach be *sincere*.

Remember, communication is a two-way situation. Someone has to talk and someone listen. You won't be able to get people to listen unless you first get their attention. And you can't get their attention until you talk about something which interests *them*. And what interests people most? Themselves. They want to discuss what they have done, what they plan to do, where they have been and what has happened to them. Never forget this!

A frequent and disastrous mistake in the art of communication is to type-cast people and talk to them on that basis. It is automatically assumed that all a woman wants to discuss is home, recipes or babies. But this is often far from the truth. Many women would prefer to talk about such diverse subjects as current events, mind power, automobiles or vintage wines. Men, too, have atypical interests. While so-called 'typical' male interests might be the stock market, football and fishing, many would rather discuss such things as cooking, crafts, art and women's rights.

It follows then that the smart thing to do is try and discover the interests of the person with whom you are conversing.

Next to talking about themselves, people like to air their opinions. It's amusing how they will discuss things about which they know absolutely nothing. Very few will admit to not having an opinion. Rather, they will create one, right there on the spot. But while this opinion may be way off base, it is important to let them express it. You will never win a friend by disagreeing with someone's opinion!

In order of importance, the next thing people like to talk about is other people. They derive real pleasure from this. Sometimes what they say has no basis in fact but, again, they are entitled to express themselves. The trick is to point out the good qualities of the person being discussed without taking exception to what is being said. While no minds may be changed, this tactic switches the conversation onto a more pleasant and positive level.

The next thing people like to discuss is things. They will talk about anything. Here is your chance to be a good listener and learn something. By doing just that, I have benefitted greatly. Even though, initially, I may have had little interest in a subject, curiosity got the better of me and I found myself wanting to know more. By listening to people who are knowledgeable in certain areas, you can become versed in and able to converse on a surprising number of topics.

The last thing people want to talk about is . . . YOU. They don't want to hear about your sickness, or your operation, or your negative views on life. Listen to yourself and note how many times you use the first-person pronoun. If it is excessive, start switching from "I" to "You!"

Keep the conversation centered on the other person. Wait until he asks about you. You can be sure that this will only be when he is ready to listen. In other words, *after* you have given him a chance to first tell you about himself. When you do talk about yourself, it should not be to draw attention to *you*, but to tie your interests in with those of the person with whom you are speaking.

HOLD ONLY POSITIVE CONVERSATIONS

We learned earlier that words have creative power, the same power as the thoughts which go into shaping our consciousness. As we are always communicating our thoughts, it goes without saying that these should be positive.

On those occasions when you, yourself, don't feel well, avoid the tendency to complain. If you are a habitual complainer, this is your way of getting attention and sympathy. Complain often enough and you will become a pain symbol to others. They will begin to avoid you for no one wants to associate with someone who makes them feel ill. Besides affecting others, you will make yourself sicker by programming your subconscious through constant repetition. A friend of mine used to say, "Never tell anyone your troubles. Half the people don't care anyway, and the other half are glad you have them!"

Talk about things which inspire others. Let them know how you enjoy life, and watch them respond. A person who sends out positive vibrations attracts people like a magnet.

Everyone wants to associate with those who have a happy and positive outlook because their attitude is contagious. Even if you feel down, pretend to feel good. You will uplift other people and, in the process, end up feeling better yourself.

Positive conversation also includes learning to keep secrets. You will gain the confidence of people in direct proportion to your ability to be discrete. Before disclosing something about someone else, ask yourself this question: "Would I tell this to fifty people?" Learn to say only those things you want to have repeated. If you use this approach, you will discover that your comments will automatically include only positive, constructive, optimistic observations.

USE PLAIN LANGUAGE

You simply cannot communicate with others unless you learn to use plain language. Something is definitely lacking in your ability to communicate if what you say cannot be understood by a child. Now this may sound ridiculous, but it is true. In my early years as a lecturer, I discovered that effective communication with my audience was directly related to how simple I could make complicated, abstract ideas.

The burden of holding someone's attention, whether it be an audience or individual, falls on you. And no one will pay attention to what they do not understand. Many college graduates cannot communicate with those on a lower educational level because they have never learned how to make things simple enough. If someone fails to understand you, it does not necessarily follow that they are stupid. More than likely, you have not explained your point clearly or simply enough. Walt Disney used animation as a means of simplification. Frequently great truths are told in parables or allegories. Let's learn a lesson from this and use simple stories, demonstrations, parables and examples to convey what we mean.

One of the best methods of determining understanding is feedback. You get feedback by asking questions like these: "Have I made myself clear?" "Do you agree?" or "What are your feelings about this?" This preliminary interchange helps develop two-way communication.

LET THE OTHER PERSON KNOW THEY ARE IMPRESSING YOU

I have already said that everyone likes to feel important. Let them know this by implying that you are impressed by what they have to say. This is done by giving them your full attention. The less you talk about yourself, the more the other person will feel that he is important. Act as if their jobs or social lives are the most fascinating things you have heard about.

I was traveling by plane on my way home from a lecture I had just given to several thousand people. I was bubbling over with excitement after an extremely successful speaking engagement. Next to me, sat a man who said he was an accountant. Well, I thought, that's a comfortable profession but how boring it must be. Of course, I didn't let him know how I felt. Instead, I listened as he talked about his travels and the complicated financial dealings of the large corporations he represented. All the way across the country, he kept me enthralled. From this experience, a great truth emerged. Although, on the surface others may appear dull, what they have to say is often more interesting and important than what we have to say ourselves.

Most people really do not communicate effectively because they are trying to *impress* rather than *express*. They engage in a sort of self-neutralizing, verbal bombardment of each other. They use words others do not understand and frequently attempt to speak down rather than *to* the person with whom they are talking. They are busy showing that person how smart they are.

Justified or not, others will form their opinions of you by the *way* you talk to them. If you show off or try to impress them with your intelligence, you can be sure that they will tune you out right away. On the other hand, if you do not talk down to them and keep their interersts and emotions in mind, they will consider you clever, interesting and, even, a brilliant conversationalist.

Studies have shown that 75% of the words you use are never heard by other people. People hear only what they want and, as you already know, the thing they most want to hear about is themselves. If you talk to them about their goals, interests, ideas, experiences or aspirations, you will immediately get their attention and continue to hold it without difficulty.

GIVE SINCERE RECOGNITION

Whenever you give your friends and associates sincere recognition, you are, in essence, showing them how to like themselves more. If you remark on something which escapes most people, you will increase your impact.

It takes little imagination to compliment someone on his appearance—although that's nice too—so the creative person looks for less obvious qualities. For example, you might notice someone's sense of humor or ability to attract friends. By taking time to remark on attributes which are far too often overlooked by others, you are saying in effect, "I really notice you as a *person*," thereby giving that person a reason to like his or herself more.

By helping others build their self-esteem and making them feel comfortable and secure, they become more friendly. This all goes back to what we said earlier: in order to think well of others, you must first think well of yourself. Knowing what pleases you and increases your self-confidence provides some excellent clues as to how you can make others feel self-confident. Someone observed, quite astutely, that when we look at our world and see God and good in everything and everyone, our world looks back at us with the same attitude.

WAIT UNTIL THE CONVERSATION GETS AROUND TO YOU

After others have talked about themselves, a point will be reached when the conversation will get around to you. A little patience here is well invested. Don't be like the actress I met at a Hollywood party who came up to me, talked on and on about her movie career and finally said, "Enough about me! How did *you* like my last picture?"

ACTIONS SPEAK LOUDER THAN WORDS

What you are speaks so loudly,
I cannot hear what you are saying.

Emerson

People will judge you by your actions. Small acts of courtesy are not just merely empty gestures, they are thoughtful expressions which say, without verbalization, "I think you are important." Unfortunately, to many, courtesy is becoming a lost art. Don't let this happen. Be one of those who still place importance on small acts of kindness which make others feel special.

It is important to realize that people are not interested in hearing us expound on our particular philosophy of life. They are more interested in seeing how our beliefs are working.

Your actions are reflections of your thinking. If others see that you are healthy, happy, prosperous and enthusiastic, they will ask what you are doing to make these things happen. There is no need to "preach" because, as the saying goes, "More Truth is caught than taught." Religious fanatics may talk about peace, love, salvation and their great happiness in religion, but all one has to do is look at their lifestyles to know just how well it's working. The Bible puts it this way, "By their fruits ye shall know them." If your life is a showcase of positive living, people will want to know how they can get on the bandwagon.

BE ON TIME FOR APPOINTMENTS

Another essential aspect in the development of good personal relationships is reliability. Being on time for appointments is more important than you realize. Lateness does not merely mean that you are irresponsible, it means that you really do not care about the person you are meeting. You are, in effect, saying that that person is not important enough for you to be on time. If you had a meeting with the President of the United States at 10:00 tomorrow morning, would you be on time? Of course. You would make a point of it. So, let's be honest. We can all be on time if we are *motivated*.

We violate the "on time" rule because we do not realize the consequences of our actions. We think we are free individuals who can do anything we want. "That's the way I am!" we say defiantly. But that's not the way we are. It's the way we have *chosen* to be. While, in most respects, it is true that we should do what is right for us first, this does not apply if something needlessly *violates the rights of others*.

Remember, then, no matter who you are meeting—executive, housewife, factory worker, secretary, salesperson, relative—or if you are attending a meeting or social gathering, *be on time*! Extend this habit to all personal relationships. Get the reputation of always being there first. If you must keep someone waiting, contact that person and explain the delay and inform him when you expect to arrive. He will admire and respect you for caring. There is nothing more upsetting and frustrating as waiting for someone who doesn't show up on time.

REMEMBER PEOPLE'S NAMES

Most of us will agree that one of the sweetest sounds is the sound of our own names. People's names are their badges of individuality so if we remember them, we automatically win their friendship. Noting and remembering a name takes only a few minutes but the investment of time and attention can bring rich rewards.

The principal reason why we don't remember names is that, when we are introduced, we don't really *listen* to what the other person is saying. If we recall the moment of meeting, the introduction probably sounded something like this: "Hello! My name is Mrkxgrtmp." We didn't hear the name correctly because we weren't paying attention. More than likely, our minds were on what *we* were going to say next!

To remember a name, first be sure to hear it properly. Then make an interest-stimulating mental impression of the total person, at the same time repeating his or her name over and over in your mind. If you remember the *whole person*, you will remember their name.

One thing you must not do is say to yourself or others, "I have trouble remembering names." By doing so, you give your subconscious a 'command' which it faithfully follows. Every time you try to remember a name, the impression is rejected because you have already stated that you cannot remember. Refute the 'command' now, and start affirming that you can remember the names of everyone you meet and recall them at will.

Remembering names should be one of the priorities on your list of self-development. *Not only will this make others feel important, it will make you more poised and self-confident.*

HOW TO MEET PEOPLE AND GET TO KNOW THEM

Don't Be Afraid To Make the First Move

Contrary to what you may believe, most people hate social gatherings. They like the idea, but dislike the prospect of meeting and mingling with strangers. If we are honest, there is not one of us who, at one time or another, hasn't felt uncomfortable at a party. The truth is that, subconsciously, we are afraid that others won't like us, and we don't want to feel rejected. It's the old need for approval springing up!

If the thought of attending a social function makes you feel, at the very least, uneasy, remember this: *you are not alone*. Many feel the same way. When you accept this as the truth, you will have a lot less trouble meeting other people.

Suppose you are at a party and don't know many people. When you look around, everyone seems to be having a good time while you are just standing there wishing you were home. But you aren't home. And there is nothing you can do about it for the moment, so you might as well make the most of the situation.

The best thing to do is to make the first move. Select someone who is not involved in conversation and appears to be alone, and walk right up to him or her. *Assume that he or she is friendly* and act as if you expect to be both welcomed and liked. With only rare exceptions, the person will react warmly and cooperate in getting the conversation going. Having taken the initiative and broken down the barriers of shyness and timidity, you will soon find your new friend talking your ear off.

Be friendly and let the conversation take its own course. Use the guidelines for communication set forth in this chapter. And don't try too hard. From the beginning, take for granted that that person will like you, and he will!

LEARN THE ART OF SMALL TALK

All conversations do not have to be heavy or philosophical. It is much better to start off a conversation with a stranger with "small talk." There is a very good reason for this. When you meet someone for the first time, they are wondering if you will be easy to talk to. The first things you say provide the answer and create the impression which sets the tone of the relationship. If, for example, you initiate a conversation with a question about someone's philosophy of life, they will be caught off guard and back off immediately. But if you start by asking *questions* about them, they will relax and the conversation will flow naturally.

If you observe television talk shows, you will notice that the host invariably starts off with simple, carefully chosen questions intended to let the guest know that the interviewer is interested in him as a person. This dispels anxiety and lets the guest talk about himself.

GET THE SMILE HABIT

A problem in communication is that people don't smile enough. Watch them on the street, at the office or even at home. How often do they smile? Some turn a smile on and off like a light switch and use it to impress others. But their insincerity is quite obvious to the onlooker. A study conducted at a major university revealed that men smile at 70% of the women and only 12% of the men with whom they come in contact. This would seem to indicate that they don't care what other men think about them but are concerned about impressing women!

Smiling is an important means of communication for it has a positive effect on others. Think how good you feel when someone smiles at you! In its simplest form, it is a way of telling you that everything's going well and that the smiler is happy to see you. Department stores have shown as much as a 20% increase in sales when employees smiled at customers.

People cannot help but warm up to a smiler. If you are not one, you had better get the habit right away. Smile right now! Go ahead! Now do it again! It doesn't hurt. As a matter of fact, it makes you feel good. If there's a mirror near by, smile and see how much better you look!

When I say that you should practice smiling in front of a mirror, I am perfectly serious. You may feel silly for a while but as frown and down-turned mouth disappear and you begin to radiate confidence and poise, your attitude will change. Every person is beautiful when he or she smiles.

You will *automatically* look and feel better. A smile is your way of writing your thoughts on your face!

A smile comes from within you so you must think positive thoughts if those are to be reflected in your smile. If you lack self-confidence or are consumed by unhappiness and doubt, you will have a difficult time smiling. The natural resistance to exposing your feelings to others will make your smile stiff and forced.

To overcome this, get to the root of your problems and change your negative self-image. Start with a smile and go on from there. Whenever you greet people SMILE! SMILE! SMILE! Smile for everyone you meet. Smile for your family, friends and co-workers. Smile for the people who frown at you. Smile in traffic. Smile on the elevator; in the store; at the bank; on the street. Smile for the janitor, the waitress, the bank teller.

Notice that I said smile *FOR*, not AT! The reason for this is obivious. When you smile *FOR* someone, you are showing sincerity. The other person will sense this and smile back. That is their way of saying, "Thanks for noticing me and making me feel important!"

Learn to *want* to smile and enjoy the happiness you bring into the lives of those who pass your way. Try smiling today and notice the magic it works. Remember, your smile is one of your greatest assets!

BE CAREFUL OF THE COMPANY YOU KEEP

Finally, be aware that YOU TAKE ON A DEFINITE PORTION OF EVERY PERSON WITH WHOM YOU ASSOCIATE. So be *very* careful of the company you keep. Make a point not only to hold positive conversations but, as much as possible, associate with only positive people. These are the people who will inspire, motivate and help you to release your unlimited potential. Negative people drain your energy with their constant putdowns and complaints about how the world has mistreated them, how their husbands or wives don't understand them, how their bosses don't value them, and how terrible they feel. Whenever possible, release these people from your life and seek out people who are uplifting and positive. Remember everyone whom you associate with affects your life.

Secret #14
ACHIEVING TOTAL SELF-CONFIDENCE THROUGH A POSITIVE MENTAL ATTITUDE

Many people believe that Positive Thinking is unrealistic because the Positive Thinker is just seeking to escape problems, tragedy and hopelessness. But this is not the case at all. Positive Thinking is a way of looking at your own problems and those of humankind and trying to solve them through constructive action. The difference between the Negative and Positive Thinker is rather like two people's reaction to half a glass of water. The Negative Person says that the glass is half empty; the Positive Person that it is half full.

Positive Thinking allows you to build on your strengths, overcome your weaknesses and tolerate your limitations. It helps you to realize that you were born to be great for, within you, is the Positive Power which can make any dream a reality. It helps you to focus on the good things in life and allows you to give your dominant attention to what is right with you, other people and the world. By seeing good around you, you generate a magnetism which attracts more good into your life. For, as we have noted, like attracts like.

But understand this. POSITIVE THINKING IS USELESS UNLESS IT PROMOTES *POSITIVE ACTION*. Thoughts or mental energy must be turned into action or kinetic energy. The kinetic energy of doing something reinforces the subconscious. And, when properly utilized, that automatic goal-producing mechanism corrects mistakes, changes courses and brings you to your target.

POSITIVE STATEMENTS RELEASE CREATIVE POWER

"In the Beginning was the Word."

The way you verbalize has a strong influence on your feelings, moods, personality, self-confidence and real life experience. Earlier, we pointed out how negative affirmations hypnotize us into failure, disappointment, confusion and ill health. So what's the solution? It is not very complicated. Just apply the reverse process. Flood your mind with power words or affirmations.

The affirmations which follow declare your strengths rather than your weaknesses. They focus your mind on the positive instead of negative; affirm what you are instead of what you are not, and what you can instead of cannot do.

Use these or similar affirmations during meditation to program your subconscious mind or whenever you find yourself thinking self-destructive thoughts.

MOVE AHEAD WITH AFFIRMATIVE THINKING

This moment affords me infinite possibilities, for I live in the eternal now of being.

Everything I can possibly be is right this moment a part of my consciousness.

This moment I am prepared and equipped to accept my limitless potential.

I am fully aware of my limitless capacity to be. My thinking is in the now; my vision is in the now; my anticipation is in the now.

My life is filled with beautiful people whose love and giving is right in my experience.

As I become more aware of my power to see, I am also more aware of my will to do.

I look to no one for my good, but recognize that everyone is a potential channel through which the Infinite can bring good into my life.

As I am complete MIND, my consciousness has in it all ideas. I know what I need to know at the instant I need to know it.

This knowing annihilates all ignorance from my subconscious mind.

I am intelligence, wisdom and love in perfect balance.

My consciousness, with its clear correct knowing, produces the desires of my heart.

This day and every day moves smoothly for me because I am confident and efficient as I allow the Divine Adequacy to motivate and activate my consciousness.

My actions are the logical outgrowth of this awareness. Success meets all my endeavors for I am adqeuate to deal with every area of my life.

I am continually receptive to new ways and methods for my greatest good.

I am creative in my approach to myself and know that the creative being that I am knows how to create from within me.

I am mentally and emotionally dedicated to my own good and to the good of others. I live in a friendly universe which responds to my healthy desires and brings them to pass.

Without conceit, I can say that I am spiritually perfect. My consciousness is healthy and I enjoy it. I have no fears and no regrets, I am vitally alive right now. I am totally self-confident.

CONCENTRATE ON WHAT'S RIGHT WITH YOU

Make a list of everything that is *right* with you. Take a good appreciative look at it. Go over it frequently. Even memorize it. By concentrating on your assets and qualities, you will develop the inner conviction that you are a worthy, competent and unique individual. Whenever you do something right, be sure to remind yourself of it and even reward yourself for the action. In this way, you will build up a new habit pattern of concentration on what is *right* with you.

In *Alice in Wonderland*, Lewis Carroll tells us how we got the way we are and how important it is to concentrate on what is right with us.

ALICE:	Where I come from, people study *what they are not good at* in order to be able to do what they are good at.
MAD HATTER:	We go around in circles here in Wonderland; but we always end up where we started. Would you mind explaining yourself?
ALICE:	Well, grownups tell us to find out what we did wrong, and never do it again.
MAD HATTER:	That's odd! It seems to me that in order to find out about something, you have to study it. And

ALICE:

when you study it, you should become better at it. Why should you want to become better at something and then never do it again? But please continue.

Nobody tells us to study the *right* things we do. We're only supposed to learn from the *wrong* first, in order to learn from that what not to do. And then, by not doing what I am not supposed to do, perhaps I'll be right. But I'd rather be right the first time, wouldn't you?

There's great truth here! Why not read it again and let it become part of your Awareness?

PRESCRIPTION FOR TOTAL SELF-CONFIDENCE

Before unveiling the finished product, the YOU it is possible to become, let us briefly go over the step-by-step process which effects this transformation.

1. Accept the fact that you are a unique individual with a place to occupy and a special purpose to fulfill.
2. Expand your Awareness and get rid of the Mis-

taken Certainties which are preventing you from releasing your Unlimited Potential.

3. To release your Unlimited Potential, choose a goal, make a plan for your life and present it to your subconscious.

4. Look within for the Divine Intelligence and Power to solve all your problems and make life as you wish it to be.

5. Visualize and affirm whatever it is you want to be, do or have in your life experience.

6. Give your Dominant Thoughts to success, not failure.

7. Master Time instead of letting Time master you.

8. Get rid of dependency, guilt, fear and worry and in their place cultivate self-reliance, love, imagination, enthusiasm, a sense of humor and the ability to communicate.

9. To help achieve peace, power and total fulfillment, practice the art of Meditation.

10. And, finally, remember that you are endowed with the ability to *choose* and the potential power to *accomplish* everything you desire.

THE NEW YOU

As you cultivate a positive mental attitude and translate that into positive action, a new, successful YOU will emerge.

You will be an individual of power, direction and planned action.

You will overcome the false beliefs which have been holding you back.

You will be a friendly person who is never lonely.

You will be a self-reliant person who controls his or her own destiny.

You will not need to judge yourself or others.

You will be a poised individual with empathy for others.

You will be open and receptive to new values, concepts and beliefs.

You will have radiant health and a longer life.

You will have a new Spiritual Awareness.

You will learn to love yourself and others more intensely than you ever have before.

A bright picture isn't it? Sure it is because it is a view of YOU once you have learned and applied the principles contained within these pages. This will take a commitment to action but will be one of the greatest adventures of your life. Once you have committed yourself to building total self-confidence you will never be the same again.

RECOMMENDED READING

Meta-physics—New
   Dimension of the Mind ..   *Anthony Norvell
                                    Parker Publishing
                                    West Nyack, NY

Self-Consistency .... Prescott Lecky
                                    Island Press, NYC

What Life Should Mean To
   You......................   Alfred Adler
                                    Grossett & Dunlap, NYC

The Fourth Way ....   P. D. Ouspensky
                              Alfred A. Knopf, NYC

The Undiscovered Self.....   C. G. Jung
                              Atlantic-Little, Brown

First & Last Freedom ......   J. Krishnamurti
                              Quest, Wheaton Ill.

Selected Writings of
Ralph Waldo Emerson .....   Ralph Waldo Emerson
                              Signet Classics, NYC

Edinburg Lectures ....   Thomas Troward
                              Dodd Mead, NYC

The Art of Selfishness .....   David Seabury
                              Science of Mind,
                              L.A., CA

Handbook to Higher
  Consciousness ....   Ken Keys
                              Cornucopia Inst.
                              St. Mary, Kentucky

Beyond Success
  & Failure ....   M. & W. Beecher
                              Pocket Books, NYC

Varieties of Religious
  Experience............... William James
                          Modern Library,
                          Westminster, MD

Power of Your
  Subconscious Mind...... Joseph Murphy
                          Prentice Hall
                          Englewood, NJ

How I Found Freedom in
  an Unfree World......... Harry Browne

Think & Grow Rich .... Napolean Hill
                          Fawcett World, NYC

Positive Living Through
  Constructive Thinking ... Emmet Fox
                          Harper & Row, NYC

Building Self-Esteem ...... *L. S. Barksdale
                          Barksdale Foundation
                          Idyllwild, CA

Psycho-Cybernetics .... Maxwell Maltz
                          Pocket Books, NYC

Science of Mind .... *Ernest Holmes
                          Science of Mind,
                          L.A., CA

All About Goals and How
   To Achieve Them ....   Jack Addington
                                 DeVross Publishers
                                 Marina del Rey, CA

What Are You?............   Imelda Shanklin
                                 Unity, Unity Village, MO

Your Erroneous Zones .....   Dr. Wayne W. Dyer
                                 Funk & Wagnalls, NY

Freeing The Whole Self ...   *Bud & Carmen Mosier
                                 Today Church
                                 Publications,
                                 Dallas, Texas

*Also excellent study courses, seminars, workshops and related material.

If they can do it,
so can you.

But first find
out *how* they did it.

Develop your success potential with these six books written by and about people who have discovered the secret of getting ahead. If you want more out of life, these books are for you!

__ 08264-4	**THE POSSIBLE DREAM** Charles Paul Conn	$2.95
__ 06306-2	**THE WINNER'S CIRCLE** Charles Paul Conn	$2.95
__ 08282-2	**THE WINNER'S EDGE** Dr. Denis Waitley	$2.95
__ 08896-0	**AN UNCOMMON FREEDOM** Charles Paul Conn	$2.95
__ 07274-6	**WITH NO FEAR OF FAILURE** Thomas J. Fatjo, Jr. and Keith Miller	$2.95

Prices may be slightly higher in Canada.

Available at your local bookstore or return this form to:

BERKLEY
Book Mailing Service
P.O. Box 690, Rockville Centre, NY 11571

Please send me the titles checked above. I enclose _____. Include 75¢ for postage and handling if one book is ordered; 25¢ per book for two or more not to exceed $1.75. California, Illinois, New York and Tennessee residents please add sales tax.

NAME_____

ADDRESS_____

CITY_____STATE/ZIP_____

(allow six weeks for delivery)   **158**

PROVEN WAYS TO
BECOME FIT AND <u>STAY</u> FIT

___ **FOOD FOR CHAMPIONS** 06771-8–$3.50
Ned Bayrd and Chris Quilter
Everything you need to know about today's nutritional
discoveries to perform at your absolute best.

___ **THE GOLD'S GYM BOOK OF** 08658-5–$3.95
STRENGTH TRAINING FOR ATHLETES
Ken Sprague
Develop your own regime at home to strengthen the
muscles you need for your favorite sport.

___ **THE GOLD'S GYM WEIGHT** 08897-9–$3.95
TRAINING BOOK
Bill Dobbins and Ken Sprague
The fast scientific way to shape your body beautiful.

___ **THE Ms. GUIDE TO** 08731-X–$4.95
A WOMAN'S HEALTH
Cynthia W. Cooke, M.D., and Susan Dworkin
The complete, authoritative guide to every aspect
of a woman's health.

Prices may be slightly higher in Canada.

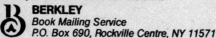